Macromedia Director: Your Personal Consultant

Macromedia Director: Your Personal Consultant

Scott Fisher

Ziff-Davis Press
Emeryville, California

Editor	Valerie Haynes Perry
Project Coordinator	Barbara Dahl
Cover Design and Illustration	Regan Honda
Book Design	Laura Lamar/MAX, San Francisco
Word Processing	Howard Blechman
Page Layout	M.D. Barrera
Indexer	Valerie Robbins
Cover copy	Sean Kelly

Ziff-Davis Press books are produced on a Macintosh computer system with the following applications: FrameMaker®, Microsoft® Word, QuarkXPress®, Adobe Illustrator®, Adobe Photoshop®, Adobe Streamline™, MacLink®Plus, Aldus® FreeHand™, Collage Plus™.

If you have comments or questions or would like to receive a free catalog, call or write:
Ziff-Davis Press
5903 Christie Avenue
Emeryville, CA 94608
1-800-688-0448

TABLE OF CONTENTS

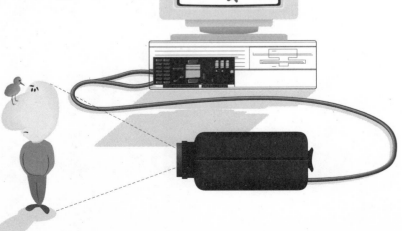

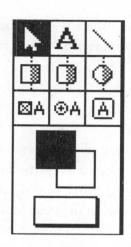

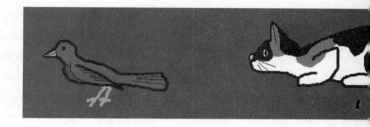

PREFACE

In the late 1940s, a new medium for communication first began making an impact on the population of America and then the world: television. The early producers of television shows saw its immediacy and its ability to reach a wide audience, and began by broadcasting live performances, much the way radio programs had been broadcast during the 1930s. The first television shows were variety acts adapted from vaudeville, as well as serious dramas such as the Hallmark Hall of Fame and Paddy Chayefsky's *Marty* (the first example of a television show that was later made into a motion picture).

By the mid-1950s, the movie industry was in disarray (compared to its strength in the Depression era) as a result of television's encroachment into the entertainment market. By the end of that decade, television was transformed as struggling movie studios, producers, and production crews applied their financially successful techniques for cranking out product to the new medium of television. The mass-produced sitcom was born, and human consciousness would never be the same.

What does this have to do with Macromedia Director? Macromedia Director is currently the most respected and most powerful mass-market tool for creating works in the new arena of interactivity, digital media, and computer-based communications. But look around you at the activity in multimedia today. It's the same situation that existed in the 1950s with television. First, television was used to adapt one existing aesthetic form to a mass-market distribution medium: stage presentations, live drama, and comedy. Later, television was used to sell products that movie studios could no longer market successfully through their traditional channels. But throughout its history, television has been used by existing media giants to maintain a kind of creative hegemony over a potentially revolutionary form of communication.

Today, much the same movement is occurring in the field of "new media." Paramount, Lucas, Time-Warner, Viacom, Compton's—all the names that you read in most stories about multimedia ventures are the same names you've read about for years in other media, either print, film, or video. We have a revolutionary way of accessing, presenting, and sharing information, a communication medium as interactive as a shaman sitting around the fire telling the myths of his people to the members of his tribe, yet at the same time as instantaneous and as universal as the six o'clock news. And yet as the medium begins to move into the future, that future is taking a depressingly familiar shape—the future of multimedia is beginning to look an awful lot like the past of television.

You can change that future, and this book will help show you how.

With Macromedia Director, a camcorder, an inexpensive digitizing card, and a few thousand dollars for distribution costs, anyone can produce sharp-looking interactive materials. The issues involved are simple, the technology is inexpensive, and the integration of different components is within the capabilities of anyone who can use a word processor and a video camera. We stand on the brink of a potential restructuring of communication on a global scale, a democratization of media to a degree that few other technical advances in the history of communication have provided.

My somewhat revolutionary contention is that the chief hindrances to this democratization of media are not technical, but creative. Knowing how to use the software isn't anywhere near as important as knowing what to use the software for. With that in mind, I've structured this book as roughly 80 percent how-to, and 20 percent what-for. I've included exercises that take you through the steps involved in importing video clips, creating animation, and adding interactivity to your title. But I've also built in examples, visualizations, and even one or two exercises that will help you tap into your own creative power in ways that I hope (and expect) will be new to you.

So as you read this book, keep in mind the following thought: This book is a challenge to you, a collection of tools and ideas that give you the power to change the world of communication and the domination of media by the few. Think television is too violent? Here's how you can make an alternative. Feel that the views of your political or cultural segment aren't being represented? Here's how you can produce an interactive presentation that addresses the issues you believe in. Or do you simply have a great product, service, or organization that you want the world and all its potential customers to know about? With interactivity, video, and animation, Director will give you a much more impact-filled presentation than any print brochure.

All you have to do is do it. It's not about knowledge; it's not about connections; it's not about understanding. It's about action. This book can give you understanding, but I hope more than that, this book can lead you into places where you can take action in your own life, in the areas of your life that you feel strongly about, where you can create something completely new, original, unique.

Whatever you can do, or dream, you can begin it: Boldness has genius, power, and magic in it.

—Goethe

ACKNOWLEDGMENTS

Valerie Perry is a great person in a great job: development editor for Ziff-Davis Press. Her insight, clarity, honesty, and perhaps most important, her composure were crucial to the degree to which this book communicates to you. I learned that if she said, "I don't get this, please explain further" about something I wrote, it wasn't her fault that she didn't get it. Any time an author finds him or herself saying, "What I really meant was," it's time for a rewrite. Valerie pointed out many—I hope all—such areas in my first drafts.

The rest of the editorial and production staff at Ziff-Davis helped me through the maze of communications programs and protocols we used to write, produce, and publish this book. Paul Freedman talked me through several different problems I was having with the online BBS; Suzanne Anthony put up with an unreasonable number of periods when my life outside this book intervened, and yet managed to keep me on something approximating a workable schedule; Barbara Dahl kept the cycle of page proofs, screen snapshots, and revisions flowing continuously during the final weeks of production.

Another person from Ziff-Davis deserves mention: Juliet Langley. Very early in the project, I made a presentation about this book at the national sales meeting. At the beginning of my presentation, there was still some confusion in the room over what Macromedia Director was all about and why people would be interested in a book about it. I spoke for several minutes about storytelling in new forms of media, about how Director lets people construct new forms of communication, about revolutionizing the creation and distribution of media. When Juliet took up my message and began explaining it excitedly to the national sales staff, I knew I could successfully infuse others with the same enthusiasm that I have for interactivity and multimedia.

Other people who provided me with examples and opportunities include Karen Savage, my personal coach, who helped me achieve a breakthrough in the way I use and relate to time; thanks, Karen. The people I mention by name in the book—Meg and Betsy Partridge, Margo Komenar, and anyone else—are all acknowledged in the context of their contributions, but are no less deserving of mention here.

Steve Chernoff of Macromedia made it possible for me to use the latest version of the product so that my readers would be up to date, and provided both the Macintosh and Windows versions of Director so that I could test some of the cross-platform issues I mention throughout the book. The staff at Macromedia in general were very supportive, even when I asked them questions in the chaos of trade shows like Macworld.

I also want to thank my many students, colleagues, and family members with whom I was able to try out ideas to see whether they worked, and on whom I could try out my explanations to see if the words were actually landing out in the audience. My wife Kim was as always a patient and attentive listener, never afraid to tell me when she was completely lost—another good sign that it's time to rewrite. And my daughter Torrey helped as well, by letting me (insisting is more like it!) teach her how to do animation with Director. When you read Chapter 4's discussion of real-time animation, bear in mind that if a seven-year-old can make cartoons on the computer, you can too.

INTRODUCTION

This book is about Macromedia Director, easily the most respected multimedia authoring tool on the market today. When I first proposed this book, there were over 100,000 Director users. When I began writing it, the number had grown to 150,000. By the time you read it, I have no doubt you'll be in the company of more than 200,000 other users of Macromedia Director. The difference, or competitive edge, between you and the other 199,999-plus users of Director is going to have to come from inside you: from gaining access to your creative vision. This book provides you with some of the keys to that vision.

Chapter 1 talks about the basics of electronic design, and introduces the concept of "interface-free design" to help you break out of the mold of designing yet another program. With Macromedia Director, you really can do something different.

Chapter 2 suggests ways you can configure your production environment to take advantage of Director's capabilities as a media integration tool. Chapter 2 also offers advice for tuning your workstation to run best with Director, additional hardware, and different monitors you might use for different kinds of projects.

Chapter 3 includes step-by-step exercises that take you through importing a video clip, making text fly over images on the screen, and changing the appearance of visual elements in your title. I also cover sprites, the way Director represents the visual elements you draw.

Chapter 4 introduces the basic techniques for animating in Director. This chapter talks about how to do simple path-based animation, real-time animation, and traditional frame-by-frame animation, as well as how to add looped movement to other animation techniques and how to construct your sprites to get the best performance out of games or other speed-dependent applications.

In Chapter 5, you'll learn the different ways you can treat text in Director. In the last section of the chapter, you'll find an exercise that will help you dive deep into your imagination to discover when words can be more magical than pictures.

Chapter 6 is about synchronizing events, such as audio and visual images. This chapter discusses Director's powerful and visually exciting transitions between frames, and suggests ways you can use these transitions to help pace your presentation.

Chapter 7 discusses true interactivity and introduces Lingo, Director's scripting language. You'll learn the seven Lingo commands you need to know to make your Director movie interactive. Even if you've never written a line of programming code in your life, follow the exercises in Chapter 7 and you will be writing successful Lingo scripts that let you create point-and-click user interfaces for the information in your Director movie.

Chapter 8 discusses a number of ways to distribute your Director title. Most of you probably assume that CD-ROM is the best choice, and for many Director titles it is. But there may be times when videotapes, disks, and/or an online site are more appropriate or cost-effective.

Chapter 9 discusses basic game theory involving metaphors for play, the concept of inventory (the loot you pick up as you play certain kinds of computer games), and how you can use games as a teaching tool or as a tool for reinforcing your marketing message.

Appendix A looks at several tools that you might use for developing prototypes of your interactive documents, and Appendix B lists some "gotchas" that new Director users sometimes encounter, as well as things to watch out for when working across platforms.

C H A P T E R

Design for Interactivity

W hat is good multimedia? For me, there is a specific as well as a general answer. The specific answer defines multimedia as a montage. This montage includes bits and pieces of all the work I've seen and enjoyed—not just on CD-ROM—but all the computer-generated imagery I've witnessed over the last ten years. This work encompasses images from motion pictures, photographs, paintings, and sketches, as well as text images drawn by words and even music.

The general answer, I hope, can be found in part in the next two hundred pages. Good multimedia is much more than a showy, flashy catalogue of your authoring system's special-effects menu. Good multimedia *moves*—not just as images on the screen, but it also stirs emotions in the viewer. Finally, good multimedia appears as seamless and effortless as good acting, good painting, or good dance. Watch Fred Astaire some time, or Bill "Bojangles" Robinson; can you *see* how hard they're working?

Good multimedia also includes interactivity, a new medium not possible outside the realm of the CD-ROM. Interactivity lets your audience change the sequence in which they perceive different parts of your story. At one level, it's a great way to look up cross-references in a training document. At a deeper level, it's an entire new art form made possible by letting the user choose his or her own path through your story, which creates a new story for each user. One way to visualize this aspect of interactivity is to consider the difference between the two sentences "What is good multimedia?" and "What good is multimedia?" Both use the same words, but by changing the order of two words, the meaning changes. Interactivity does the same thing but at the level of paragraphs or of scenes in a motion picture. By changing when something happens for the viewer, you change what happens just as surely as if you change "What is good multimedia?" to "What good is multimedia?"

Throughout this book, I'll propose a wealth of ideas that I hope will help you recognize and create good multimedia. At its heart, good multimedia combines all forms of communication into one interactive feast. The trick is to make that feast a banquet.

In this chapter, we'll look at what interactivity really means, some of its possible long-term effects as an entertainment and educational medium, and how you can maximize the element of interactivity to give additional power, effectiveness, and excitement to your titles.

Who Uses Multimedia?

You use multimedia, but who are you?

It's practically universal for an author of technical books to open by identifying his or her audience. The common wisdom says this will help potential buyers recognize themselves and be more willing to plunk down their hard-earned dollars on that counter in the bookstore. I have a different reason for identifying who I think you are: Perhaps some of you don't know yourselves.

You probably think you're information designers, developing multimedia titles for entertainment, education, corporate marketing, schools, professional clients, or maybe even just for fun. Well, here's a surprise: That's not who you really are. Sure, that may be how you categorize yourself, and "information designer" may be a good description of what you do on a daily basis—but as a user of Macromedia Director at this stage of the multimedia industry, you are really someone quite different. You are actually the inventor of a new future, a future in which among other things the words "computer-literate" are meaningless, because this label applies to almost everyone.

The average computer user has been trained to have certain expectations about using the computer, the most fundamental of which is that computers are fun. And that's who I think we are—we're the people who can make using computers fun, easy, self-training, and powerful enough for even a three-year-old to use. I know this from experience because when my youngest daughter was three-and-a-half, she was already able to access the File menu and Quit command, even though she couldn't read the words! She learned them easily as a part of having fun with the computer. Multimedia stands to make nearly any application on the computer enough fun that anyone can figure out the controls for themselves.

What Is Director and What Can It Do for You?

Director lets you create, combine, and display moving images on the computer, and allows your users to control what displays and when. It does this with a degree of detail and precision that other programs can't begin to match.

Interactivity isn't Director's real strength; I know half a dozen programs that offer interactivity with far less effort. Nor does Director's main strength lay in its ability to combine video with text and graphics. Framemaker, for example, does a superb job of that, and does it very simply. And though Director provides two different cross-platform solutions—you can develop on the Macintosh and use Director's player for Windows, or you can develop directly on a Windows PC—even that isn't its real strength. Director's real power is that it can do all of this 60 times a second. Director's 2D (two-dimensional) drawing capabilities are pretty sophisticated, but they're nothing compared to Director's ability to put these drawings up on the screen at whatever frame rate your playback system can support.

Animation, like any other kind of film or video, effectively stretches layout over time. In creating a visual document, not only does animation allow you to present images in the familiar dimensions of 2D and 3D, but effectively in four dimensions as well. You can change the contents of the screen, which defines a context for your users. And because of the interactivity that Lingo (Director's scripting language, covered in Chapter 7) provides, you can set up an almost unlimited number of possible contexts, depending on which path your users take into the fourth dimension.

Director is essentially a new kind of program, a combination of layout, interactivity, and synthesis. It's a tool that lets you combine disparate elements into a single unified presentation; it's also a tool that lets you define ways in which the user interacts with these elements; and of course, it's a tool that lets you lay out the individual screens that present your users with the possibilities you have envisioned for each screen in your title. And one of the new possibilities, a possibility that didn't exist before interactivity and the new medium that it permits, is the possibility of user-defined context, which is covered later in this chapter.

Interactivity: The Space between the Spokes

There's a verse by Lao-Tzu, the Chinese philosopher and author of the *Tao-te Ching,* in which he talks about how 32 spokes converge in the hub of a wheel, but the usefulness of the wheel comes from the space between the spokes. Likewise, the real power of multimedia does not come from the fact that you can merge text, video, animation, sound, graphics, and motion all in the same presentation. Videotapes have been doing that, to a vast market, since the widespread acceptance of the VCR more than 15 years ago. What really gives computer-based, or digital multimedia, its power is the user's ability to interact with it: to control it, to select from it, to go from one location to another and come up with a new thought that arises from the juxtaposition of two ideas in the work. Just as the questions,

"What is good multimedia?" and "What good is multimedia?" use the same words in a different sequence to convey completely different meanings, so does interactivity itself make possible new meanings from the same story components. This shift is accomplished by letting the users define their own context, as a composer creates a new melody using the same 88 notes on the piano keyboard.

Real creativity, or for that matter real intelligence in any form, comes from the ability to connect two given facts, two known pieces of information, and come up with an unimagined, unexpected connection as a result. Fundamentally, this is what computer-based interactivity is all about.

Interactivity involves the ability to follow a path through a network of connections that spans a wealth of information. Furthermore, these links must be established within seconds of issuing the command. The technology that makes this possible lends a power, speed, and effectiveness to computer-based media that has never before existed in human history. You can arrange it so that as your audience is thinking about something, you can connect them with a different but related piece of information at a distant part of your document. In doing so, you make possible an explosion of nonlinear learning that is potentially limitless in its ability to change how people learn, how they relate to their world, and most importantly, how they create projects.

In some senses, then, layout is the physical representation of interactivity. It presents the choices with which the user can interact; it filters the user's available interactions, based on the artist's perceptions and skills. Are there any fundamental physiological principles that you can adopt as a basis for layout? Are there rules for layout of information that can help guide people through your presentations in ways that will make them smarter and you richer? The answer, of course, is "sort of." There are guidelines you can follow to make your Director presentations as effective as they are exciting.

Guidelines for Developing Presentations

Most of the human-factors research is well documented elsewhere; I cover much of it in my other books and in the classes I teach. To recap in the briefest possible way, here are the hard-and-fast rules:

- Short-term memory can contain five facts, plus or minus two, for 15 to 30 seconds before it needs reminding. This gives a good rule of thumb for how much information to put in a slide, on a screen, on a portion of a menu, or in some other chunk of a user interface.

- The eye itself does not follow any predictable path through a page (or screen) design. Research with eye cameras—that is, with a camera that checked the position of the readers' eyes while they were browsing in a magazine (the medium of choice for this research, documented by Allen Hurlburt in *Layout: The Design of the Printed Page,* Watson-Guptill, 1977)—noted only that the eye tends to alight first in the rough center of a layout, then make a kind of ragged, spiraling star around disparate elements of the page, unless it's following some known convention.

- Finally, memory consists of three phases: acquisition, storage, and retrieval. *Acquisition* is the experience you have that causes you to remember something, for whatever reason. *Storage* determines how you remember what you've decided you should; it's the act of inserting a memory into your store of knowledge in such a way, and in such a structure, that you can recall it again when called upon to do so. And that, of course, leads to the final panel of the triptych: *retrieval,* your ability to come up with the memory on demand. Retrieval is based to some extent on storage, which is the purpose of mnemonic tricks (such as the old "every good boy deserves favor," used to teach music students that the lines in a staff stood for the notes EGBDF). If you store information in a manner that makes it easy to locate, particularly by combining a number of senses at once, you'll be more sure of retrieving the information later when required.

And that's about it. The rest is pretty much all convention, expectations, aesthetic choices, or other elements that are entirely up to the individual designer.

This is either good news or bad news, depending on your orientation. If you're looking for advice on how to make your presentation easier to learn, about how to lay out your interface in ways that the human eye naturally follows, you'll still have to rely on good design, rather than on some physiological magic bullet, to help you through. On the other hand, it gives you the freedom to do what you think is right (and, perhaps, the documentation to prove in a design meeting that your way is as good as the ones you're competing with).

Whether you're designing a presentation for eventual use on a PC or a Macintosh (Director 4.0 lets you author on both platforms) you may find some good insights in the Macintosh User Interface guidelines published by Apple Computer. If you don't want to do that, see the sidebar, "Using Screen Real Estate Wisely," for a few basic suggestions.

Using Screen Real Estate Wisely

Users have certain expectations about the arrangement of their computer screens. The upper-left corner is where people look for global controls: It's where the Mac and Windows menus both put the File commands, for instance (and it's why my young daughter knew where to move the mouse to select Quit). The lower corners have specific meanings as well for most users: You click on the lower-right corner to go to the next screen, and clicking on the lower-left corner takes you to the previous screen. Keep in mind that this is by no means a hard and fast rule; the best-selling CD-ROM to date, *Myst,* uses a completely different sense of screen geography. Above all, be true to your own aesthetic vision.

Note also that the positioning of information on the screen moves out of the visual realm and into the *kinesthetic* realm—the realm of motion and position. Educators sometimes characterize learning abilities as visual, verbal, and kinesthetic. Kinesthetic learners acquire knowledge through the position and motion of their bodies, or at least use the sense of position and motion as a way to store and retrieve information. So, in a subtle way, by making users move the mouse to different locations on the screen, you're reinforcing learning. In fact, you may even be reaching individuals who are kinesthetic learners—just as including audio helps you reach verbal learners and including graphics helps you reach visual learners.

In addition to managing the user's attention as he or she accesses individual screens, there are some fairly standard techniques that you can use to ensure the usability of the interface to your document. And one of the best ways to do that may be to let go of the notion that you're designing an interface to your document. It's a technique that I call "interface-free design," admittedly not without controversy.

"Interface-free" Design

How can multimedia design be interface-free? Isn't everything we do with a computer, and specifically with a multimedia title, part of the interface? Of course it is. Now forget you knew that, and let's start fresh: Remember, inventing a new future means more than just working on a graphical presentation for a client or publishing a CD-ROM entertainment title.

It was during a discussion with Brian Blum, producer of the CD-ROM title *How Multimedia Computers Work*, that I first came up with the term "interface-free design." Brian opposed the characterization because he thinks of himself as "an interface designer." Therefore, he couldn't see a design without an interface as something worthwhile. Of course he's right, at one level. His interface is beautiful, elegant, sophisticated, and thoughtful; his design is anything but interface-free.

One way to characterize this term is to consider the differences between something like a Broderbund Living Book on the one hand, and Microsoft's Encarta on the other: Encarta looks cluttered and cliched, like a computer program, while a Living Book doesn't *look like* an interface: It looks like the thing it represents.

So of course, there's no such thing as interface-free design. The very best user interfaces simply require no additional effort to learn; they imitate the subject that they represent. This reinforces learning in both directions: As users become more familiar with the subject, they also become more familiar with the document, and vice versa. I sometimes say you should strive to make your designs look like they have no more interface than a pastrami and Swiss on rye, that they're as natural to use as a knife and fork (or, in my household anyway, chopsticks). The most engaging CD-ROMs, such as the phenomenally successful *Myst,* owe a big portion of their blockbuster status to their "interface-free" presentations. More than any other examples of multimedia I've seen so far, these programs enable the audience to lose itself in the presentation. Users are able to forget they're using a computer, playing a game, learning, being trained, or whatever the objective may be for a particular CD-ROM.

Using Layout as an Information Channel

Successful multimedia developers begin with the concept of layout (borrowed from traditional visual design) but modify the concept to take into account time, motion, and interactivity. If it's carefully planned, this moving, selectable layout can convey a subtle, additional information channel on top of the traditional media of text, graphics, and sound.

Your document's layout (the appearance of each screen, and the way you position objects on each of your screens) can actually guide your users through the document. Intelligent consistency that is followed or violated intentionally and for effect can direct your users' attention to specific areas. This consistency can suggest a logical or dynamic flow within the screen; it can draw attention to or from a particular area of the display; and it can also serve as a navigation tool. Layout for interactive documents can do all of these things, but it's also dynamic: It can change as a result of user interaction. In effect, your document's layout becomes your title's user interface, at a very deep level.

Note: I will generally use the word "document" to describe what you're working on, and "title" to mean what you hope people will flock to the stores to purchase (or, more realistically, your end product). The two words are almost, but not quite, interchangeable; one multimedia title may have several documents, which in turn may be made up of a number of different files on your computer.

In summary, layout becomes an information channel of its own, in addition to the obvious channels of text, video, audio, and graphics. The position, location, size, and structure of elements on the screen can convey information to your audience. By carefully constructing each screen for its information content as well as its aesthetic look, you can instantly convey information about your title, your subject, or the structure of the section while your reader is at work.

Procedural Layout   One of the differences between multimedia and traditional media is that multimedia's information changes (or at least can change) with the direction that the user takes within the a document. The principles of procedural layout and relative importance are key considerations for user-defined context as a layout guide.

Figure 1.1 shows one of the simplest examples of the principle of procedural layout. You can see the whole presentation with the current section of information highlighted. There are two ways to achieve this effect. In this illustration, the clip shows the steps involved in making a traditional holiday recipe, love knot buns. Thumbnails down the side of the display show the overall sequence, and clicking on each of them will display the video for that step in the process.

The inherent procedure implied by the top-to-bottom presentation of the four thumbnails (reinforced by the numbers superimposed over them) makes it apparent that this layout represents a procedure. You can use a similar scheme to represent a hierarchical layout, in which the uppermost images are meant to comprise the lower and subsequent images—or rather, the sequences of media that those images represent.

Figure 1.1
Video recipes:
love knot buns

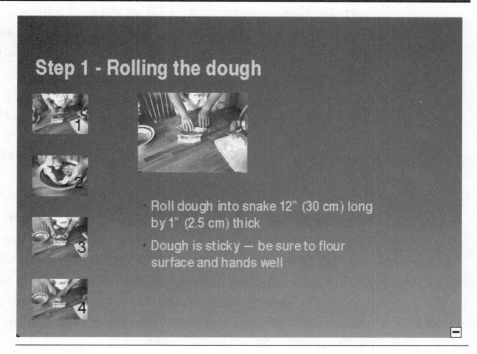

Relative Importance   In addition to showing sequence by layout, you can show the relative importance of various pieces of information in your document. Size and screen placement can let users know the relationship between components of a screen. You may wish to couple this with other visual cues, such as graying-out some screens, that indicate when the user has already read screens.

Lee Leth, president of The Knowledge Organizer and developer/ designer of information interfaces since 1980, started me thinking about what he called a "taxonomic index." He uses this term to define a way of presenting cross-references to different portions of a document in some manner that would indicate the relative significance of each entry in the index. This influenced the design of what I call IntellAssist, a text-based navigator that I've used in several electronic documents to connect related subjects. As tempting as it is to use visual representations for all kinds of information, there are still times when text is the most compact, the most easily interpreted, and the most unambiguous medium. Often, specific kinds of navigation work best with text. Figure 1.2 shows an example of how text can indicate the relative importance of several cross-references. This kind of multidirectional popup index solves a number of problems in laying out information on a screen. The knottiest problem is what to do when a hot-spot might take the user to any of several different locations.

Users of Windows help systems have likely seen lists of "See Also" jumps to related sections of the help file. They consist mostly of text, they break the flow of the narrative (when there is a narrative flow), and they take up screen real estate whether the user wants to look at them or not. Consider putting this kind of information into its own popup subwindow; the main context remains visible on the full-size window beneath the list of cross-references, and you can even put the cross-references themselves into a scrolling region if you have a lot of them.

Best of all, for users of Director, is that while I designed IntellAssist to solve the problem of multidirectional hypertext links in electronic publishing, it solves a fundamental information problem independent of medium. Because it appears when context demands, and because it appears in the form of a user-selectable option, IntellAssist doesn't have to take up room on a display until you (or your user)

Figure 1.2
A typical
IntellAssist
navigation
panel

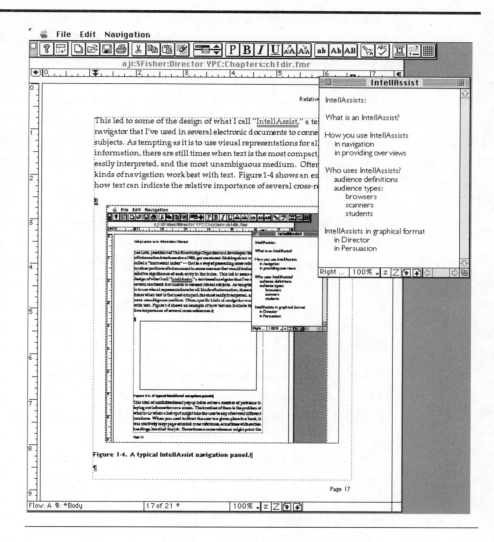

need it. In this way, it's a layout technique that is dependent on the information content, and which furthermore varies with time.

I recently talked with Meg and Betsy Partridge, filmmakers and CD-ROM designers for a series of titles on American women photographers. They plan to use the IntellAssist approach on some of their upcoming projects within the context of a video clip or some other time-dependent medium (such as narration timed to still photographs). "When we want our users to make connections between different parts of a film," said Betsy, "we can have something like this popup to let our users know there's more information out there."

At present, IntellAssist needs comparatively old-fashioned record keeping: You simply have to know where the information is, then build the popup modules to let your users know where else they can look for related pieces of information. The first book-length project on which I used IntellAssist already existed as a paper book; you can take advantage of some of my experiences by tracking these references (and more importantly, you can track the places in your document that require the references) while you are still developing the work. I'm still evolving the best way to track them; so far we've used the traditional technique of white boards and Post-It notes, a printout of the document with blank facing pages to make notes, and a hybrid paper-electronic database that seems the most promising. Obviously, a little custom software development is in order.

Prototyping: Checking Your Layout As odd as it may sound in a book dedicated to Director, one way you may be able to save time in developing Director titles is to develop prototypes with a simpler (though perhaps less capable) program, such as Aldus Persuasion or AltaVista MediaWrangler. Prototypes are a great example of one of my favorite aphorisms: Every day spent thinking about a project before you start working saves four days spent working on it before you start thinking.

Prototyping bridges the gap between thinking about a project and working on it. Not only does it put your thoughts into a concrete form you can play with, it also allows you to share information with others working on the same project. Chapter 9 covers some details about techniques and tools you may find useful for doing storyboards, animatics, and other early tests without spending so much time on the job that you end up wasting effort. Chances are you already do storyboards for your projects. They're the logical place to start developing the jumps and destinations in your interactivity. If you're not already marking places in individual scenes, frames, or illustrations that you intend to use as jumps to other locations in your title, begin now. If you don't really understand how to design for interactivity yet, keep reading this book.

You need to track the flow from one portion of your title to the destination when your user clicks on a link. What you look for at either end of the link will differ depending on the kind of title you're developing. If you're putting together an encyclopedia-like title, such as a tour of the zoo, you'll want to make sure there's a smooth transition of tone, topic, and assumed knowledge across the jump. If you're putting together a game, you'll want to manage the transition in such a way that your players won't get lost between the source module and the destination module. And if you're checking the flow from the table of contents to the individual modules in your title, you need to make sure that the title picks up at the beginning of the destination module. Whatever kind of document you're designing, check it, test it, and most importantly, have someone else test it. You'll be surprised at what you've taken for granted after having seen the silly thing for 12 hours a day.

This means when you pick a prototyping tool, make sure you pick one that provides you with some way of adding interactivity to your prototype. For example, although Microsoft PowerPoint is a fast way of putting video, flying text, and other appearances of multimedia into your presentations, it doesn't (at least in its current release) let you specify hot-spots on the screen. Persuasion does, and it does so in a very simple way.

Perhaps the biggest argument in favor of prototyping your Director titles with Persuasion or MediaWrangler is that you can begin testing, editing, and verifying your project's flow quickly, within a day or two for many documents or for pieces of complex titles. Then you can send a simple working prototype to your Lingo programming staff (or to consultants you hire specifically to write the Lingo portion of your title) to design the full Director treatment for your finished title. Both Persuasion and MediaWrangler offer "point-and-click" interactivity: They let you define regions on a screen (rectangles in the case of Persuasion, polygons with up to 255 vertices for MediaWrangler) by drawing them with the mouse, and then specifying another image to be displayed when the user clicks the mouse inside the region you've defined.

It's important to start prototyping your interactivity early for the reasons already mentioned: What your users get out of your title will be determined largely by their ability to track their work from topic to topic. In fact, Director's real power comes from its ability to jump from topic to topic, to let the user pause at any subject long enough to comprehend it, and to provide you with the ability to connect any two ideas in the document that you think will interest your users. It's very important to construct your document in such a way that the connections between these ideas are clear, easy to identify, and easy to track down again later. Like the space between the spokes, inter-activity provides an unseen benefit between the concrete portions of your title.

Review: Time, Context, and Creativity

In this chapter, we've looked at a couple of suggested techniques and examples for laying out the screens of your Director titles. Most importantly, we've had a chance to explore how layout changes in the context of multimedia. This change is evident not only in the impact that time and time-dependent media have on appearance and content, but also in the impact of interactivity. When your users define their own context dynamically as they use the document, you need to reflect this in the document's layout. In that sense, the layout itself becomes a fifth channel of information, in addition to text, audio, graphics, and motion.

In the next chapter, we'll take a look at some of the essential equipment (both hardware and software) for developing titles with Director, as well as at a few interesting toys that make life easier or more fun, while perhaps not being essential.

CHAPTER

2

Configuring Your Production Environment

Where does Director fit into the hierarchy of multimedia productions? Because of Director's power, it doesn't have a single place in your production environment, but rather occupies any of a number of positions along a continuum of possibilities. In the early parts of this chapter, we'll look at some of those possibilities. Then we'll examine some additional aspects of your environment—other pieces of electronic equipment, special software packages, and even to some extent additional staff (or at least additional skills) you may want to consider to achieve the vision you have for your multimedia title.

The Multimedia Production Environment

Fundamentally, Director offers a range of features that fall somewhere between two extremes: a high-powered animation program, and a fully flexible integration tool. At one end, Director is a tremendously powerful animation program. It gives you the ability to do frame-by-frame movies, offering precise location of graphical elements on the screen, and permitting superb control of pictures in place and time. You can think of this aspect of Director as "MacPaint for flip books": It lets you do anything you can do in a typical draw and paint program, but it also gives you the ability to display your images up to 120 times per second. At this end of the spectrum, you could create what amounts to a computer cartoon, a piece of pure animation in which you draw every image using Director's tools and use no outside media components whatsoever. A talented artist could create a powerful multimedia title in just this way, using nothing but Director's innate drawing, animation, and sequencing tools.

At the other end of its feature continuum, Director is a fabulously powerful integration tool, giving you a great way to combine disparate graphical elements such as QuickTime movies, video

111111

clips, and sound effects that come from external applications or special hardware. To take an imaginary title from this end of the production spectrum, it's possible to create a powerful, effective, and beautiful presentation that uses no visual elements created inside Director itself, but in which Director simply provides the staging, the context, and the playback for visual elements, sounds, and text developed entirely in external applications.

The Design Team

You probably work as part of a team. This is generally a safe assumption if only because there's so much work to be done in title development, and splitting it among more than one pair of hands helps get it finished. Furthermore, the specialization required for each medium means that your titles will look, sound, feel, and perform better if you find a team whose skills complement one another. In some ways, the design team is the most important element of your production environment, and the one you should spend the most time, thought, and energy configuring.

You probably work cross-platform at least some of the time. In a few years, the PC may be as mature a development platform as the Macintosh, or the decision to release clones may make the Macintosh as ubiquitous as the PC. But for the time being, the chances are good that you develop on the Apple and port to Windows sometime later. With two-thirds of the multimedia player market being Windows-based, it's hard to pass up the chance to go for so many millions of potential buyers, even for dedicated Macintosh partisans. Likewise, with the seamlessness that the Mac gives to media elements traveling between applications and across peripherals, and with the way it just does what you want it to do without having to reconfigure the BIOS (most of the time, anyway), the Macintosh remains the development platform of choice for a significant number of developers.

You probably want to include at least some video in your title. Animation is wonderful and you can do great things with it, but for any audience over the age of about nine, video images make the difference between something that looks like a cartridge-based game and something that looks like a television show. If you're developing games or edutainment for really young children, they may actually prefer all-animated titles to titles with video in them. For adults, video better conveys a process, or the results of change over time. For example, in a multimedia presentation designed to teach a surgical procedure, you might include animation describing what the procedure was meant to accomplish. However, video of a surgeon performing it would be irreplaceable.

You probably don't have an unlimited budget. As much as I hope this book provides exceptional value for the money, if you had an unlimited budget you could hire an actual consultant, who would probably charge you what you spent on this book in the first 15 minutes. There's no shame in being on a budget; in some ways, I think I'm proudest of the cheap, sneaky, and impossibly clever ways I've come up with to get interesting images into my books and CD-ROMs without spending thousands of dollars on equipment. My favorite one involves using one of the modules from a screen saver to make what looked like a chalk picture of a video frame; it made a stunning background that always got comments, and yet I had made it with part of a package I'd bought for $29.95.

The Range of Interactivity

Imagine a graph that represents all possible Director titles, with two axes: One axis shows how much of the title's content was generated in Director, and the other axis shows how much content was imported from other media such as video (see Figure 2.1). Lingo scripts provide you the range of interactivity. Essentially for every point on the continuum between pure animation and pure integration, you can choose a point along another axis that spans the capability for interaction. At one end of this axis, there's no interactivity beyond running the program, and at the other, every visual element on the screen is a button.

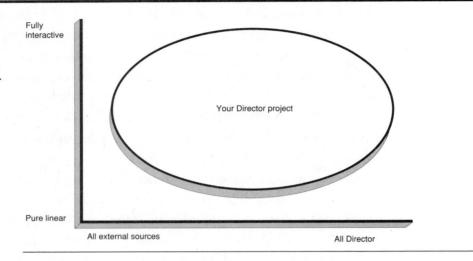

Figure 2.1
The range of multimedia titles possible with Director

Fully interactive

Your Director project

Pure linear

All external sources

All Director

While your Director project will fall somewhere in the space created by the intersection of these two axes, this chapter addresses some of the concerns that affect where you want to place your project along the horizontal axis: how much media you import from the outside world.

Fine-Tuning Your Workstation

A friend of mine says, "Having all the trick stuff won't do you a bit of good if it doesn't work together." That statement is most true when it comes to integrating a computer system. This section discusses how to get the most out of your production environment, even if you never plan to use any tools other than Director for multimedia development.

System Integration

It's been my experience lately that more work is involved in integrating different configurations of PCs than in porting between the PC and the Macintosh. For example, video capture cards require their own interrupts, which potentially conflict with sound cards or other peripherals; DLLs load over each other; system drivers are incompatible; video overlay cards won't work in certain monitor resolutions; and the list goes on. Even the Apple world isn't immune to these problems. Here's a case in point: RasterOps makes a video overlay card for the Duo Dock PowerBook which requires its own system extension. But if you take the portable Duo out of the dock, it hangs up and refuses to start unless you power-cycle and then restart with extensions off. However, the Extension Manager, included in System 7.5, lets you choose from all your available applications (or predetermined custom sets of them) if you hold down the space bar while the PowerBook starts.

Maximizing Performance

The good news is there are some safe combinations, such as the Sound Blaster CD-16 sound card, which everyone tests for and with which virtually all applications claim compatibility. But whether you're talking about testing for user compatibility or simply trying to get maximum performance out of your workstation, be certain that all your components, hardware and software, work together. Even then, there are a few tricks for maximizing performance during video capture and compression:

- Turn off virtual memory. You don't want the system paging in the middle of compressing a video clip. (This is another argument in favor of buying extra RAM, up to 24MB if you're planning to do a lot of video capture and compression.)

- On the Mac, turn off AppleTalk. AppleTalk polls its devices frequently, causing a degradation of compression performance.

- Put a CD-ROM in the drive and a disk in the floppy drive. On the Mac, at any rate, both of these devices are polled regularly until you put something in; once you insert a disk or CD-ROM, the system stops checking to see if you've done anything.

- Turn off your screen saver. I love my After Dark screens, but that program checks the mouse 60 times per second. And if for some reason the screen saver were to come on—for example, if you started compressing a video clip, then walked away to make a pot of coffee—your frame rate would plummet.

- Use fast disk drives, AV drives if possible. The disk response speed should be as high as possible—meaning the response time should be under 10 ms, as far under as you can find.

In recent months I've seen specialized AV drives. Ordinarily, disk drives fragment the file so that it's distributed evenly around the surface in uniformly-sized units called *extents*; these extents are normally as noncontiguous as possible to make system response time fairly consistent when reading text and data files. AV drives, on the other hand, are optimized for recording (and playing back) media such as audio and video, where the chunks of file are larger and by nature more contiguous. Also, most AV drives are designed not to do a thermal calibration in the middle of a write. Thermal calibration is performed by all drives, and is necessary to keep the read-write head in proper synchronization with the disk surface as the components change temperature. An AV drive disables thermal calibration during writes, because the calibration itself takes a fraction of a processor cycle—again, not enough to notice when you're reading or writing text with a word processor or calculating a spreadsheet, but enough to make a jump or a hiccup in a piece of captured video.

Beyond those listed above, there are additional devices, options, accessories, and software packages that are handy if you're planning to use Director to create more than a few multimedia titles.

Processing Power

For multimedia developers, high-performance processors aren't a luxury, they're an economic must. Your computer's processing speed has a direct impact on how soon you can bill your customer for your time, or on when you can deliver the finished products to be put on CD-ROM and shipped to waiting customers. Speed is a critical factor in rendering 3D animations, compressing video, calculating in-betweens for a piece of animation, or performing any other computation-intensive operation. Put in that light, a few hundred dollars for a faster CPU doesn't seem like such an outrageous expense. If you're using the machine to make money, a faster machine will make money faster. It's that simple.

Having said that, you can do a lot of good quality work on relatively inexpensive equipment. The mainstays of my studio are a pair of low-priced machines, a Macintosh Quadra 630 and a Compaq Presario 860. Both use 33/66 MHz chips and both provide adequate (if not blazing) performance for most of the operations I put them through. These two machines sell for about the same price—well under $2,000 in today's market, with CD-ROM drive, 8MB of RAM, 13-inch monitors and identical 340MB IDE hard drives. They'd be excellent choices for prototyping stations, for layout and design artists, and for low-cost workstations in general multimedia development. Yes, if you buy a Pentium 100 or a Power Macintosh 8100AV you'll capture video more quickly, you'll render 3D graphics more effectively, and you'll run performance-sapping applications like Framemaker, Photoshop, and Director even more quickly. But you can get a reasonable amount of performance for about $2,000 at today's prices, and you can always either upgrade the equipment later or you can give it to new staff when you buy yourself a supercharged machine after the royalty checks start rolling in.

There are a few things to watch out for, however, if you're planning to purchase additional workstations at the lowest prices. First, as much as I like my Quadra 630, it uses a 68LC040 chip, and you need to know that while the official designation of the LC version of the Motorola 68040 is that it's the "low cost" version, my own mnemonic is that "LC" really stands for "lacks coprocessor." I installed a 3D rendering package on my 630 some time ago, only to learn when I tried to run it that this particular software requires a coprocessor or a Power Macintosh to run. That doesn't mean that it runs slowly if you don't have a 68040 or a Power PC—it means that when you double-click on it, it tells you it can't run and then it quits. Fortunately, I was able to borrow an 8100 for the project, and the program in question (Logomotion by Specular) uses QuickTime as its output medium, so I could still composite my presentation on the 630 using QuickTime files.

In the PC world, you're going to drink a lot of coffee if you have anything less than a 486 with the fastest clock speed you can buy. (A Pentium-based system may or may not be better depending on when the chip was made; there's a good likelihood that complex animations may encounter the specific floating-point error that the Great Bug of 1994 made infamous.) Of the various 486 devices, the primary tradeoffs are whether you go for clock speed or bus speed. A friend at Intel reported that in his own comparison benchmarks, a 50 MHz chip with a 50 MHz bus and adequate cache memory outperformed a 66 MHz chip with a 33 MHz bus.

Memory Considerations

Never mind what the box says: You shouldn't plan to use Director effectively on a machine with less than 8MB of RAM. Sixteen is better, and 24 better still, but 8MB will get you in the door. You'll be compromising the size and complexity of the images you load, however, and you'll have to adopt a less efficient strategy for using multiple applications if you plan to use additional programs with Director.

Having additional memory on the Mac or the PC means that you can have more than one program open at the same time. In the Mac's Multifinder, you can open an image processing program like Adobe Photoshop or a drawing program like Illustrator, manipulate an image, then copy it onto the Clipboard and paste it into Director easily. Yes, you can do this if you have to shut down the image program in order to open Director because there isn't enough RAM to run both programs at once, but you have to do this for every image you want to copy into Director from the external application. This gets tiresome after the fifteenth or twentieth illustration—and if you're retouching images that you plan to use as the frames of an animation, that's only a couple of seconds worth of cut-and-paste operations. The sensible thing to do is to use the Import feature of Director to pull in files, especially multiple-frame animation files. But the ability to switch back and forth between programs without having to save and exit, then start the next application, can be a huge time saver.

Adding cache RAM for 486-based machines with slower bus speeds (below 50 MHz) will also speed up throughput. The cache is an area of RAM dedicated to storing prefetched instructions and data for use in a program, in an area that can be more rapidly accessed than in system RAM. Machines with less blazing speed in the system bus benefit particularly from higher quantities of cache RAM. As with so many pieces of advice, buy as much as you can afford.

Storage Alternatives

Where are you going to keep these fabulous files you're working on? One of the smartest ideas I've adopted recently is to use my system's internal hard drives as application storage. Additionally, I use external, multigigabyte storage for keeping the raw video files, large images, and other space-intensive media that go into multimedia development. Both my studio systems have internal 340MB IDE drives, which give a reasonable amount of room for a fairly serious complement of multimedia development tools (Director, Illustrator, Photoshop, Photostyler, Framemaker, Persuasion, and a number of others). Meanwhile, I've been able to take advantage of the drop in disk drive prices to save hundreds on the purchase of a couple of gigabytes of external disk space.

SyQuest Drives

If you're working across platforms, storage is an intermediate form of transfer. The simplest example of this is when you copy a flattened QuickTime movie to a PC-formatted disk in your Mac's superdrive, then insert that disk into the PC and watch the movie with QuickTime for Windows. But it's easy to develop QuickTime movies that exceed the 1.44MB limit of a single floppy disk. You've got several options, beginning at about $200 (as of January 1995, at any rate; prices may continue to drop) for a 44MB SyQuest removable-media hard drive.

SyQuest drives have become the de facto standard for working with most service bureaus. Unfortunately, like all companies that have to continue to grow in a market of relatively fixed size, you have some decisions to make regarding which SyQuest drive you acquire. There are two sizes and several densities; the older technology uses 5.25-inch cartridges that can store either 44MB or 88MB, depending on the type of drive you purchase; the 88MB drives can read and format 44MB cartridges to ensure compatibility with older versions of the product. In the last year or so, SyQuest has introduced a 3.5-inch drive that can format and read three different densities of cartridges: 100MB, 200MB, and 270MB.

Many people I know use SyQuest drives as a backup system (a topic I cover in a few pages), while I use mine primarily as a way of transferring video clips or PostScript files to printers, service bureaus, and World Wide Web sites. Your intended use for a SyQuest drive should help you determine which size and what density to purchase. If you're mainly interested in using your SyQuest to communicate with printers, service bureaus, and publishers, go with either an 88 or a 44; this is the most established size, and you will have no trouble communicating with most places that use Syquests for transfer. An 88 will give you the ability to store more data on a single cartridge if you're using it for backup (meaning fewer cartridges to store the entire contents of your 340MB hard drive), while still letting you read and format 44MB cartridges for use with facilities that have older equipment.

If you're working only with cutting-edge bureaus, or if you're mainly interested in using the SyQuest as a way of storing backup copies or rotating the stock of your projects and you care less about compatibility with a wide range of other facilities, the 3.5-inch drive gives you a number of benefits, starting with smaller footprint. Let me assure you that footprint is an issue, though my favorite space-saving trick is to put the 44MB SyQuest drive under my PC's monitor, which is resting on my VHS tape player. This frees up enough room to get both keyboards on the desk at the same time if necessary.

Other benefits of the 3.5-inch SyQuest are simply that the smaller cartridges store a lot more data. One 270MB cartridge can hold almost half the data that you can put on a CD-ROM, meaning that this is an easy way to transfer the Macintosh or the Windows portion of a CD-ROM to the service bureau when you're cutting ISO-9660 masters. Even a 100MB cartridge holds more than the higher-density 5.25-inch drive permits.

Other Storage Options

Other storage options you might consider as part of a backup strategy include Bernoulli drives (which are functionally similar to SyQuest drives), magneto-optical (MO) drives, digital audio tape (DAT), and other tape-backup systems. If you're interested in transferring your files to another site or a service bureau, these are probably not as universal as Syquests.

CD-R Drives

But for a truly universal storage, transfer, backup, and even delivery medium, look into CD-Recordable (CD-R) drives. The prices have plummeted and will drop even further. In 1993, CD-ROM masters cost $2,000 each and were made on machines that cost as much as $40,000. At the end of 1994, I saw an advertisement for a multisession CD-R drive for $1,800. Friends in the industry have told me to expect prices in the $600 range by the first quarter of 1996.

If you're looking for CD-R as a backup, distribution, and storage solution, you need to remember a few basics. First, of course, is that it's a read-only disk when you're done with it; you can't erase it and use it again and again as you can with magnetic media. However, this makes it a great solution for taking snapshots of released, published material that you may wish to store for archival purposes once you've finished developing it.

I specified a multisession CD-R drive above, and while there are a number of reasons why they are better, you may be able to get by with a single-session CD-R system for backup, transfer, and similar applications. A multisession CD-R system lets you write information to the disk at several times; a single session CD-R system "freezes" the disk surface after the first (and only) write. Multisession drives are useful for making copies of material from more than one computer, for instance, or for making cumulative records. (For example, some educators are looking into using multisession CD-R systems to

Summarizing Your Storage Requirements

Give thought to the kinds of media you're planning to use. Images and image libraries can take up hundreds of megabytes in rapid time, and video is the worst as it has a new image every fifteenth of a second or even more often. Several digital video consultants I know recommend at least 2 gigabytes (that's 2,000 megabytes) of storage as a minimum for doing production digital video work. Fortunately, the cost of storage keeps dropping, and at today's prices an external 2.1GB SCSI device runs about $1,000. (It's hard to imagine that at the end of 1992, I paid an additional $100 to upgrade my Macintosh Classic's internal hard drive to 80MB, from 40MB, because an external 40MB hard drive cost $600. Today, that same money would buy me more than 42 times as much storage.) But if you're doing mostly small images with complex scripting—say, lots of characters that the user moves to different places on a few screens, with little or no complex imagery, animation, or video—you may be able to get by without much more than your system's internal drives.

Give thought to the uses you have for your storage. You can sometimes, especially in smaller organizations, find more justification for buying a piece of equipment if there's more than one use for it—or more than one user. Ask other departments if they'd be willing to split the cost on something like a CD-R system; your MIS people might be interested in using it as a backup system, your technical support department might want to use it to burn updates to the product, and other groups in your organization may be able to chip in a little from their budget. Even more crucial, though, is to consider ways to use the same piece of equipment for more than one purpose, let alone more than one project. A Syquest drive will be much more cost-effective if you use it for communicating with vendors (many printing shops rely on them for transmitting images, PostScript files, and other material that gets turned into paper) than if you do nothing but make backups or move files around.

Look ahead, but not too far ahead. It's tempting to buy the most you can afford today, but the reality in the storage market is that you can save hundreds of dollars—thousands if you have more than one system for which you're purchasing the equipment—by waiting a few months. The only justification most people use for buying new equipment today is the consideration of window of opportunity; when you know that you can save several hundred dollars by waiting till the end of the quarter, you have to justify spending that extra money now in terms of how much sooner you can finish (and therefore either bill for or start selling) a project. Time really is money, in this case the amount of either that you save or spend in order to hit the moving target of multimedia development. At the same time, don't plan for the needs of this week, or even this month; work has a way of expanding to fill the storage space allotted for it. So plan on growth, on additional projects, and additional needs for high-volume media images. You or your artists will come up with justifications fast enough.

store the cumulative transcripts of students' academic careers on a single CD-ROM that they could carry with them from year to year.)

Beyond Director: Add-on Hardware and Software

Processing, memory, and storage are all issues that affect the entire spectrum of Director projects, at least as I laid them out in Figure 2.1. But what about special accessories that let you incorporate other media, other kinds of images, or other effects in your titles? Having looked at the kind of equipment you might want to consider for a pure Director title development project, let's take a look at some of the features you might like to include in a title that incorporates video, digital photographs, and cross-platform development.

Video Capture

Fundamentally, video capture is simple. You need a camera, a capture card (or an AV Macintosh), associated cables, and lots of disk storage space as outlined in the preceding section. Figure 2.2 shows the basic setup in schematic form.

Where it gets complicated is in the possible options you can choose from. My capture experience covers a huge price range but a fairly small number of systems: the Apple Video System (about $250), the Intel Smart Video Recorder Pro (about $550), and the Radius VideoVision Studio (about $3,500).

Certain applications may find a digital camera, such as the Apple QuickTake (about $600), to be useful. I, however, find that the combination of a high-quality camcorder and a capture card to be more flexible, for about the same price, because the camcorder lets me capture moving images as well as stills.

The big issue, of course, is resolution. If you never plan to print your images, or at least if you never intend them to be anything more than screen snapshots in a manual or a book, you can get by with video

Figure 2.2
The parts of a
digital video
capture
system

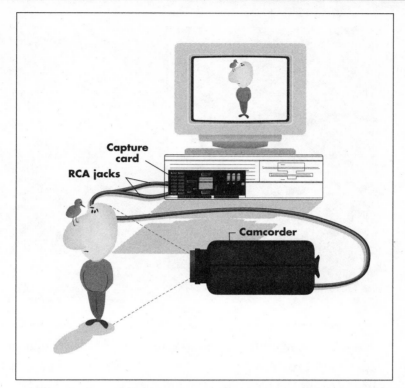

resolution. In the United States, that resolution is 640 pixels by 480
pixels (PAL and SECAM are only slightly different), and there are various ways of achieving that size. Figure 2.3 shows a screen snapshot
into which I've embedded two smaller versions of the same picture.

These images are all taken from the same piece of video, captured
with the Apple Video System on a Quadra 630. This system captures
pictures at varying sizes and resolutions. The medium-sized picture
is the best clarity and resolution that the Apple Video System provides; it's 320 pixels wide by 240 pixels high, or ¼ of a whole NTSC
screen. This is the largest image that this capture card can display in
hardware; the full size image is achieved by duplicating every pixel
horizontally and vertically, to fill out the full 640 by 480 NTSC

Figure 2.3
Video window
size, clarity,
and resolution

screen. (I've used this to good effect by filtering the double-pixel images in Photoshop, particularly if you use some of the more unusual filters provided by Xaos.) The smallest picture is 160 by 120 pixels, and is achieved by undersampling (that is, taking every other pixel) from the medium picture.

Print resolution varies; if you're planning to output to a high-resolution laser printer (at 600 dpi), these images look reasonably good, especially if you start with the middle image and play with the pixel density (Frame is particularly good at this). If you're planning to release a coffee-table art book to go along with your CD-ROM, you will need a high-priced digital camera (expect to pay about $10,000 for a decent one). Such a camera, however, will give you the same image quality you could get from film, but with direct output to a highresolution digital image.

QuickTime: Incorporating Digital Video

If you're planning to incorporate digital video into your title, you've got more important things to do than worry about resolution: You've got playback speed to consider. Most important: If you haven't yet got QuickTime 2.0 for the Macintosh developers among you, get it. In some ways it's more important than the kind of video capture card you get. Here is a comparison of QuickTime versions 1.0, 1.6, and 2.0, looking at the image sizes and frame rates they support:

QuickTime Version	Image Size	Frame Rate
1.0	160 × 120	10 fps
1.6	240 × 180	12 fps
2.0	240 × 180	30 fps
	320 × 240	15 fps

A crucial feature about the frame rate/image size pairs in version 2.0 is that this works out to 300 kilobits per second, which is the transfer rate of double-speed CD-ROM drives. (Single-speed drives run only at 150 kbps). So if you're developing video with CD-ROM as your delivery vehicle, QuickTime 2.0 is your friend.

What about the Windows side of things? Video For Windows 1.1 is the logical solution for native Windows applications, and if you're planning to go cross-platform, it's possible to go from VFW to QuickTime in software.

Macintosh developers looking to expand into the Windows market have always liked Director. It's even easier now to include video, because QuickTime for Windows makes it possible to develop video on the Mac, save in the appropriate format, and play the same files on Windows systems at QuickTime frame rates. If you don't already have the QuickTime Developer's Kit from Apple, consider spending $195 on it for the complete cross-platform solution. The crucial components are MoviePlayer 2.0, which lets you save QuickTime movies in QuickTime for Windows format. Furthermore, this product is compatible with Windows's Object Linking and Embedding (OLE), meaning that you can develop applications that run QuickTime movies on Windows platforms just as you can import QuickTime into a Macintosh document. But of course, that's part of the beauty of Director: It does all that for you.

Presenting Adobe Premiere

If you're serious about using digital video, Adobe Premiere is easily the most respected desktop video editing package in the business. If you have enough memory and disk space to support the image depth, you can store full 30 fps digital movies, do AB-roll edits (that is, combine images from two separate video sequences into a single output stream), manage overlay effects, trim frames to make cuts precise and smooth from sequence to sequence, and handle special wipes and transitions. The best way to put it is to say that Premiere is to video editing software what Director is to multimedia authoring software. Both are the results of commitments to doing things the right way. Just remember that full-screen, full-motion video uses approximately 30 megabytes per second—and that's if you use frames instead of fields. This works out to about 30 seconds per gigabyte, or (at today's prices) about $900 a minute for storage.

Premiere is also available for both the PC and Macintosh platforms.

Sharing Files between Macs and PCs

If you're developing with a mix of Macintoshes and PCs, you need to remember that no matter how easy it is to read PC disks in post-System 7 Macintoshes, eventually swapping floppies won't cut it. Sooner or later, no matter how carefully you think you trim things, you'll end up with a video file that's larger than 1.4MB. (It doesn't take much—using the smallest window and the highest compression on the simplest Apple compression card, you cross the 1.4MB boundary in less than a minute of 15 fps, 160 by 120 video with poorly synchronized sound.)

The cross-platform network world is expensive if you want an easy solution, or fussy if you want a cheap one. Farallon's EtherWave transceivers aren't inexpensive, at about $100 per system, and they really work best in a client-server world (for instance, with a Sun workstation acting as the file server and with PCs and Macs hooked up to the Sun). But they do let you drag and drop files from the central file server to either the Macintosh or the PC, regardless of file size (within the limits of the free disk space, of course). The Farralon solution is typical, and one that I'm familiar with; it's reliable, seems to configure easily, and is a good way to get Macs, PCs, and Unix machines all sharing files as required.

The bargain solution is MacLink, a PC-to-Macintosh null modem cable with software that runs on both ends. It lets you copy files from one machine to the other, it's fast, and it's easy to use. If you've only got two or three machines and you don't require regular, transparent access to files from any of a number of platforms, MacLink is a fast way to shoot big files across the wire. At about $100, it's a reasonable way to get things from one platform to the next. The MacLink Plus software translates from PC to Macintosh format for a number of popular applications, such as Framemaker, Word, Adobe Photoshop, and the unbelievably flexible SimpleText, which is now how Apple stores QuickTime movies.

You can also send large files by modem, if you have multiple phone lines for each of the computers to use. Again, this isn't a good solution if you have a team of five or six people who have to access the files regularly, but if you follow the develop-move-port approach to cross-platform development (that is, you get a working, completed version on one system, then transfer the files to the other and make minor—one hopes—adjustments to the document on the destination platform), there are a number of inexpensive X modem and Z modem protocol packages available, most of which come bundled these days with high-speed modems.

Monitors: NTSC, RGB, and Size

If you're planning to use Director to develop presentations that people will see on television, on VHS tape, or on some other medium that uses NTSC video as its final display format, you should have an NTSC monitor somewhere in your studio. NTSC colors and RGB-monitor colors look different, because the components are mixed differently and use a different color model. If color matters to you (and if it doesn't to you, it will to your clients), you need to check your presentations in NTSC before you make thousands of copies of a videotape to give away at trade shows.

Monitor Size

Other than that, you may want to make sure that you develop on 13-inch monitors, at least part of the time. Why? Not just because it saves you money, but because you'll be sure to develop in an environment that duplicates what most of your customers will have. I do some of my development on a Radius 21-inch two-page display, some on a PowerBook, some on the 13-inch Super VGA monitor hooked up to my 486, and some on the Macintosh Color Display on the 630. I like the two-page display best when I need to get in and bump lines a pixel or two, when I want to feather something, or when I want to look at a two-page spread (which is a concept that doesn't apply to Director). But there's a big difference between the size of the window in my 21-inch Radius and the size of the active matrix display on my 280. Most Macintoshes are smart enough to adapt the display to fit the window, but in the PC world, I'd be nervous. And even then, it's still a good idea to get a feel for what your product will look like on the typical monitor size.

Other than that, there's always a reason to have a bigger monitor, even if you are only going to develop for PowerBook displays. The added precision that a double-size monitor gives you is extremely valuable, especially for animation where a few pixels one way or another in something like the expression on a character's face can make all the difference in the finished output. You will probably also want some kind of non-mouse input device for doing your drawing; one graphic artist, on her first exposure to drawing with a mouse, called it "like painting with a bar of soap."

With these pieces of advice out of the way, let's jump into the deep end of Director development: the end of the spectrum that relies on media captured from the real world. Sound, video, and motion are the core of any multimedia presentation, and the next chapter discusses how Director handles them, and how you can make them work for you.

CHAPTER

3

Moving Pictures, Flying Titles

Multimedia has been around since Egyptian hieroglyphics, which after all combined pictures and text. *The Book of Kells,* Ireland's great treasure of medieval art, mixes illuminated letters with beautifully crafted text for what is surely an unsurpassed blending of words and pictures. Of course, there's one thing missing from both hieroglyphics and *The Book of Kells* from the standpoint of media: Their media don't move.

Moving pictures have been around only for about 100 years, since Edison figured out how to make gears move the frames of a roll of film and synchronize the frame rate with a shutter. The first movies, in fact, combined text with moving graphics—pictures of people, animals, cars, trains, or whatever the story was about, interspersed with slides of text to tell elements of the story that the picture alone could not.

About 30 years after Edison invented both the moving picture and the phonograph, Western Electric developed a practical way of synchronizing sound and motion, and thereby invented the first multisensory multimedia. There are two pieces of historical trivia that are related to that development. Western Electric was associated with what is now Bellcore, Bell Communications Research, which has become one of the computer industry's foremost advanced research centers. The other is that one of the first lines of spoken dialog from the first commercial talking motion picture, Al Jolson's *The Jazz Singer* in 1927, was "You ain't heard nothin' yet!"

In the past two chapters, I've talked about how Director can take a position in the hierarchy of production as an integration tool. As such, it relies on content provided by other software tools, and often by other team members. This chapter outlines how to use Director best with a variety of external software types and standards; it also provides an overview of the sources for multimedia projects.

Making Movies with the QuickTime System Extension

For video, there are two standards that Director works with: Quick-Time and Video for Windows (which is stored with the file extension .AVI). Because QuickTime is available on both Macintosh and PC platforms, I tend to talk about it more often than I talk about AVI files. However, most of what I say about using QuickTime movies for cross-platform work in Director also applies to using .AVI files for PC-only titles. Because these technologies are so crucial to adding real-world images, sound, and sensation to your Director titles, it's worth taking a moment to explore them before we get into the hands-on section of this chapter.

To make QuickTime movies, you need a digitizer of some kind, such as those described in Chapter 2. The output of these digitizers are streams of data that make up the series of frames in a movie. These data frames include stereo sound as well as picture information. In turn, the QuickTime system extension keeps the sound and pictures synchronized as closely as possible given the available performance of the machine on which your QuickTime movies eventually run. In fact, QuickTime is the best way to ensure the tightest possible synchronization between sound and action, especially for longer clips and longer sounds. Sound always plays back at a rate very close to real time; video may sometimes slow up, because a slower processor may not be able to decompress (or for that matter copy from disk) all the frames in a document while it is running other tasks at the same time.

There are other ways of recording sounds on the Macintosh or the PC. For example, you can use the Macintosh internal microphone to get sound effects into your system. You can also copy from audio CDs, from digital audio tape, or by capturing a sound-only Quick-Time movie. Additionally, you can extract just the sound track from a QuickTime movie and use it as the narration or sound effects for

Apple's QuickTime system extension consists of a standard format for compressing, storing, and playing back digital movies. This standard format is backed up by modules required by the system software to support QuickTime playback in Macintosh and Windows applications. Many people confuse QuickTime with a program you can run, but it's more like Adobe's PostScript printing language, which also combines a standard interface with software modules included in other applications. Both QuickTime and PostScript make possible a standard output across platforms and applications.

your visuals. Because the sound portion of a QuickTime movie is usually much, much smaller than the visuals, consider producing a trailer or teaser on disk as an inexpensive way of advertising your CD-ROM title. You could incorporate the same sounds, use still images (which take up much less room), and still use Director to provide synchronized playback, interactivity, and the "look and feel" of your title, all using excerpts from the same media.

QuickTime for Windows

In 1994, Apple Computer released QuickTime for Windows (QT4W), a system extension that brought QuickTime to PC users. With QT4W you can simply convert all your Apple QuickTime movies to run on the PC.

The key to this is a program called MoviePlayer 2.0 from Apple Computer. MoviePlayer "flattens" your QuickTime movies, making them playable on non-Apple systems. When you select Save As from the MoviePlayer, you get the following dialog box:

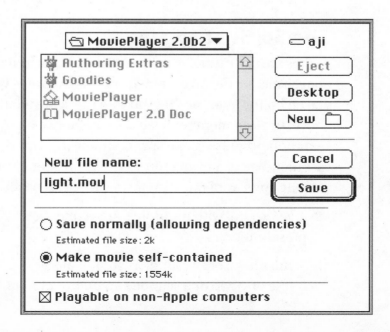

The key is to select the radio button labeled "Make movie self-contained," and then check the box at the bottom of the screen marked "Playable on non-Apple computers." Next, give the new file a name that is eight or fewer characters long plus the file extension .MOV. You will be able to play this movie on either Apple or Windows systems. (As an added bonus, the public-domain program xanim permits playback of QuickTime movies on Unix workstations as well.)

Manipulating Cast Members

To get the most out of Director, you need to understand Director's mechanism for moving cast members on the screen. When you put a cast member on a particular location, Director doesn't actually move the file itself there: It copies that cast member's *image* to the location you specify. This copy of the image is known as a sprite. If you put the drawing in a different location, change its size, or otherwise alter the appearance of your character on the Director stage, Director changes the sprite, not the cast member.

The Spirit of Sprites

Sprites are the means by which Director manipulates the moving images in a scene. All cast members have sprites when they're placed on the stage or dragged into the score window. As mentioned above, the cast member itself does not move on the stage as the presentation progresses; the sprite, which is a copy of the image of the cast member, is moved around as the presentation plays.

In the context of this chapter, a sprite can be any of the following:

■ A video clip, with multiple frames that display in sequence as the presentation runs

■ A still image of any kind, including pieces cut out of a digitized frame of video or a scanned-in photograph or PhotoCD

■ Custom artwork created in Director or in any other illustration program, such as Adobe Illustrator or Photoshop

In addition to having control over the sprite's position on the stage in the two dimensions of height and breadth, you can control the sprite's position in the dimension of depth and also in the dimension of time. In this case, depth determines whether an object appears in front of or behind other objects in the scene.

Directing Sprites

To put a sprite on the stage, you can do one of two things: drag the desired cast member into the stage and put the member in the desired location for the frame you want, or drag the member into the Score window and put it into the frame and channel you want. Both techniques put the cast member's sprite on the stage and in the score so that you can control where the member appears and when things happen to it. However, dragging the member directly into the Score window (see Figure 3.1) lets you control with greater precision the

Figure 3.1
The Director Score window, with frames across and channels down the display. Although a Macintosh is shown, the Windows version is similar.

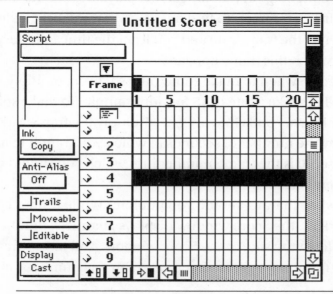

time and depth at which the member appears in the scene. This method also lets you manipulate what objects in the scene will draw in front of the cast member and behind it.

For best control over time and depth, then, get into the habit of dragging the cast member into the Score window, not onto the stage. When you drag a cast member into the Score window, you automatically get a finer degree of control over when and where (in depth) the sprite will appear. If you place the cast member on the stage, Director puts it into the next available channel and does so at whatever frame you had selected last. This may give you the values you want, but it can also surprise you. If you get into the habit of putting your cast members into the score instead of onto the stage, you'll always know when they appear and what will be in front of or behind them.

How you manage this is relatively simple. Director manipulates the time at which sprites are visible by the frame numbers that appear across the Score window. Frames located toward the left of the window are displayed before frames located toward the right. Director keeps adding new frame numbers as you need them. Whenever a cast member's number appears in the frame, that cast member appears on the stage at that time in the playback—at the time indicated by the frame number. To find out when that will be, divide the frame number by the frame rate and you'll get the time into the presentation at which this frame appears.

To decide when to make something show up, multiply instead of divide. Let's take a rate of 15 fps, for example. To make something appear four seconds into a scene, multiply the frame rate you are using by the number of seconds at which you want it to appear. In this case, 60 is the frame number into which you should drag the cast member.

But what channel should you put it in? While frames count from left to right, the Score window displays channels, numbered from 1 to 48, down the side of the Score window. And just as frames with higher numbers appear after those with low numbers, channels with higher numbers (those closer to the bottom of the display) appear in front of those with lower numbers (those closer to the top of the display).

Once you have your sprites positioned where and when you want them to appear in depth and time, you can drag them to the location on the stage at which you want them to display. Every time Director creates a sprite on the stage, it automatically gives it a bounding box and *handles*—the rectangular outline with little squares at the corners and in the middle of each side. To move the sprite where you want it on the stage, simply grab the sprite somewhere inside the bounding box and drag it to the location on the stage where you want it to appear.

Moving Sprites during Playback

You can also move sprites around on the stage during playback. This means, for example, that you can import a video clip and have it (or still frames from it) move around on the screen while the action goes on. The smoothest and easiest way to do this is with Director's path-based animation feature.

While Chapter 4 discusses Director's animation features in more detail, it's worth talking about path-based animation here because it lets you move captured images around on the screen easily and with a high degree of finesse. Path-based animation works the most effectively if you drag the cast member into the frame and channel you want, then use the In-between Linear option of the Score menu to create the animation.

Placing a Video Clip in Your Document

Using a video clip in a Director document involves three basic steps:

■ Importing the video clip

- Positioning the clip in the score

- Making the clip visible in its entirety

Here are detailed instructions for each stage of the process:

1. *Importing the video clip.* To import a clip, pull down the File menu and select Import. Director displays the following dialog box:

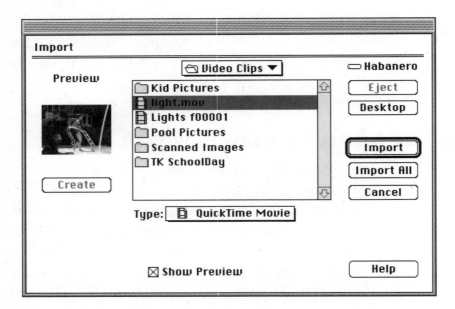

At first, the Type pull-down will display PICT. Put the cursor in the box, pull down and select QuickTime movie. (This is also how you import graphics generated by other programs, such as sketches done in Adobe Illustrator or digital photographs manipulated by Adobe Photoshop.) When you have selected the video clip you want, click Import. Director will add it to the next available slot in the Cast window.

2. *Positioning the clip in the score.* For now, select frame 1 in channel 4. The channel numbers determine what is in front of or behind the image you are working with; channel 4 will leave you three channels to put in background images later.

To move the video into frame 1 of channel 4, drag from the Cast window to frame 1 in channel 4, then let go of the mouse button. Director now adds the Cast member's number to that frame in the score.

3. *Making the clip visible in its entirety.* This step requires a little thought but not much work. You have to know the frame rate of your document and the duration of the clip. For example, a 4-second video clip in a 15-fps document requires 60 frames ($4 \times 15 = 60$). Note that this is independent of the frame rate or playback speed of the video clip: If you have slower video, Director automatically fills in the intermediate frames in the procedure below.

To see the whole movie, you need to tell Director to put the Cast member that contains the movie into every frame in which you want it to be visible. The easiest way to do that for video is to put the Cast member into the first and last frames in which it will be seen, then let Director fill in the frames between these two extremes.

You've already determined that your four-second clip needs to oc- cupy frames 1 through 60. You also dragged the Cast member into frame 1 in step 2 above. Now drag it into frame 60.

As it stands, Director will play the first frame of the movie and the last frame of the movie, with blank screen between them for 3.88 seconds. Here's how to make the movie visible between the first and last frames:

1. Click on frame 1 in channel 4. This selects the first frame of your movie.

2. Scroll to frame 60 in channel 4, then hold down the Shift key while you click on it. Director highlights all the frames in chan- nel 4 between 1 and 60, inclusive.

3. Press Command-B to determine the frames between the two ends. Director then fills frames 2 through 59 with the Cast member you have selected for frames 1 and 60. When you play your movie, the video will be visible in each frame of the Director document.

4. Watch your movie! To do this, press the following three keys:

- Command-1 to expose the stage

- Command-R to rewind your Director movie to the first frame

- Command-P to play the movie

You can add frames if your clip was slightly more than four seconds long; simply follow the same procedures just given in steps 2 and 3, but make the presentation long enough to include all your video.

Moving and Expanding a Video Window

Because sprites can be video clips as well as still graphics, you can do interesting effects with moving, panning, and zooming in or out on the video clip while it plays. Remember that the video will always look sharpest at the resolution at which you digitized it. However, if you plan to zoom in or out on a clip, you'll want to shrink it down to the smaller size and either begin (for zoom-in) or end (for zoom-out) at that modified size.

Here's how you can make an imported video clip start in one corner of the screen, sweep down to the opposite diagonal, and zoom to full size in one simple operation. (For the clearest example of the following procedure, pick a large-format video clip—one at half-NTSC resolution (320 by 240) or higher.)

1. Import a video clip: Pull down on the File menu and select Import.

By default, the Type box is set to PICT (for the Macintosh) when you first use this dialog box. Pull down and select QuickTime Movie for this exercise; Director then displays files of that type (and folders) in the selection pane.

When you have chosen a video clip, click Import and Director adds the video clip to the next available member of your file's Cast window.

2. Add the video clip to the score by dragging the clip from its location in the Cast window to a frame in one of the open channels of your Score window. Select the first frame in a channel that is closer to the bottom of the screen than any other channel.

3. With the first frame selected, choose a beginning size and location for the clip. For this exercise, drag the video clip up to the upper-left corner of the Stage. Grab the lower-right corner of the window and shrink it to about one-fourth its original size.

4. Drag the cast member into the last frame you want Director to display. You can determine this by clicking on the Information button of the Cast window (the button with the lower-case "i" in it). The following information displays:

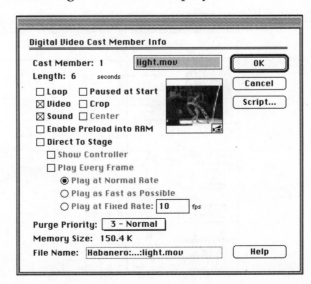

Multiply the length in seconds times the number of frames per second to determine the frame number into which you need to drag the clip. For a 15-fps movie, shown here with a length of 6 seconds, your last frame would be frame 90.

5. With the last frame selected, choose an ending location for the clip. For this example, drag the clip to the lower right-hand corner of the stage. Leave it at full-size to maximize image clarity.

6. Select all frames between the first and last frames of this clip. The easiest way to do this is to click on the last frame (since it should still be visible), then use the horizontal scroll bar in the Stage window to view the first frame. When you can see the first frame in the Stage window, hold down the Shift key and click the frame. (On the PC, use the left mouse button.) This selects and highlights all the frames between 1 and 90, in this example.

7. Fill in the in-between frames. Director does this automatically if you press Command-B. Alternatively, you can pull down the Score menu and select In-between Linear. Director fills in the frames between 1 and 90 with the number that corresponds to this cast member (in the example here, 01):

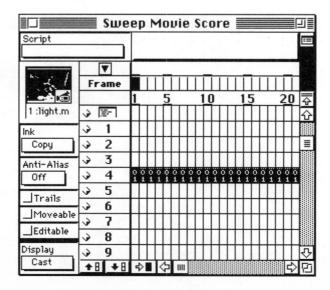

8. Watch your movie! Get into the rhythm of pressing Command-1, Command-R, and Command-P as if you were playing a melody on the piano. These commands do the following:

- Command-1 clears the screen and displays only the Stage; the Score, Cast, and Control windows disappear (as does the Macintosh menu bar).

- Command-R rewinds your movie to the first frame. (Same as clicking the Rewind icon in the Control window, but that window is invisible because of the Command-1 keystroke.)

- Command-P plays your movie. (Same as clicking the Play icon in the Control window, but that window is invisible because of the Command-1 keystroke.)

You should see your movie sweep from the upper left corner of the screen down to the bottom right corner, and grow from one-fourth its initial size to full resolution.

That's the basic procedure for making sprites move and change size on the screen. Save your file; in the next section we'll make another screen element appear on top of it.

Sprites and Inks

We've talked about sprites, the images of some element of your cast. Director draws sprites on the screen to control how your visual elements appear; you saw how you could shrink the sprite and move it around without changing your original video clip. You can also change the way sprites appear by changing what Director calls the "ink" with which you draw the sprite.

Of course, it's not really ink. The ink selection in Director specifies how the image of your sprite is drawn on top of the scene beneath it. In that sense it's like an ink, but an ink that can be transparent in places, can have soft edges, or can otherwise change the way it interacts with the image that's underneath it.

While there are some great "special effect" inks in Director, the three that you'll probably use the most are

- **Copy** This ink simply copies the sprite's image directly into the location in the screen that you have selected for drawing it, as though pasting a rectangular sticker on top of the underlying graphics. Copy is useful for regularly shaped images such as video frames, buttons, and the like.

- **Matte** This ink follows the outline of an irregularly shaped piece of art. Where Copy puts the whole rectangle into the scene, Matte follows the outlines of the parts you have drawn, as though you had cut it out with an X-Acto knife and laid it onto an art board. This ink is useful for drawing characters, for pasting in images cut out from video or scanned photographs, or for moving other opaque but irregularly shaped images around the screen.

- **Bkgnd Transparent** Like Matte, this ink follows the outline of the object, no matter how irregularly it's shaped. However, Bkgnd (short for background) Transparent also cuts out any places inside your sprite where the background shows up as white in the original drawn image.

The last two will give you the most power and effectiveness, particularly when you draw text over the screen.

Figure 3.2 shows the difference between Matte and Transparent. Both examples in this figure show the same cast member, the words "Ferrari 275GTB" as they appear on the stage. The top example uses the Matte ink; notice how the holes inside the letters (the closed spaces in the "e" and "a," for instance) and the trapped spaces between the text and the art beneath it remain white.

Figure 3.2
The difference between Matte and Bkgnd Transparent inks

That's how Matte works: It follows the outline of the text and the graphic beneath it (drawn together as a single Cast member), but leaves any other background elements set to white. This is a useful ink style for moving 1-bit sprites around on the stage, which gives you the best performance; for instance, if you draw just the outline of an object, add detail lines inside it as though you were doing a pen-and-ink drawing, but want to keep the white areas opaque, this is the ink to use. Director will "cut out" your line drawing, but leave the white highlights inside the figure as you move it around the screen.

Bkgnd Transparent ink, on the other hand, starts out like Matte but also removes the background color (in this case, white) from the spaces inside the letters and trapped inside the graphic. If you're moving text over a dark background, Bkgnd Transparent is the ink to use. This process is discussed later in this chapter.

Other Ink Styles

Now that you've seen how to change ink styles, and seen examples of when you might use the Copy, Matte, and Bkgnd Transparent styles, play around with the other styles. "Darkest" and "Lightest" have potential as ways of "graying out" a video window or a graphical element, to signify that your users have selected them from a menu or a display. Some of the other ink styles present themselves as interesting special effects—you can do interesting drop-shadow, highlight, or even halo effects by putting one graphical element on top of another that's a small percent larger or just offset by a couple of pixels from the topmost image.

Making Text Move Over Video

In the last exercise, we moved a video clip across the screen diagonally and had it expand from quarter-size to full resolution. In this exercise, we'll add a "fly-on" to the same scene: a text element appearing from off-camera and moving into position in the center of the stage.

1. Make sure Director is running and that the file you were working on previously is open.

2. Create a text element to display in your scene. To do this, select an empty cast member and press Command-5. This opens the Draw window. Click the A in the toolbar on the left of the screen to specify text entry. For this exercise, type the words "Eggplant Parmigiana" into the box that appears when you clicked the A. (You may or may not like to eat it, but it has lots of trapped areas inside the Gs, the Ps, and the As.) Select a font you like, set the size to something large like 36 points, and pick a bright color.

3. Find frame 1 in the Score window. To do this, use the horizontal scroll bar to move all the way to the left.

4. Find an empty channel with a number higher than the channel used for your video clip. You want the text to appear over the video while it's in motion, so you need to select a channel that

has a higher number (that is, one closer to the bottom of the screen) than the channel in which your video clip is animated.

5. Drag the text element into frame 1. The text appears in the center of the stage.

6. Position the text element where you want it to begin. For this exercise, drag the text element down to the bottom of the stage so that it is invisible in frame 1.

7. Find the last frame of your presentation. Use the horizontal scroll bar across the bottom of the Score window to locate the last frame that has a Cast member's number in it.

8. Drag the text element into the channel you have selected for it. Drop the Cast member into the Score window, selecting the last frame in the same channel you had previously used for your "Eggplant Parmigiana." The text appears in the middle of the Stage.

9. Animate the text fly-on. Just as you did with the video, select the last frame in the Score, scroll left to find the first frame of the channel with "Eggplant" in it, then hold down the Shift key and click the mouse button over frame 1. This selects all the intermediate frames. To make Director fill in the in-between frames with the starting and ending positions you have selected, press Command-B. The Cast member number for your "Eggplant Parmigiana" appears in every highlighted frame.

10. Watch your movie! Remember, Command-1, Command-R, and Command-P is the "tune" you play to clear the stage, rewind the movie, and play it.

Now you get to play Siskel and Ebert (or Lyons and Medved if you prefer). What does it look like? When does the text cross the video image? And how come it's got so much white space around the letters? That white space, of course, is there because when you first create a text element, Director selects Copy as the default ink. Later on, Director will retain the last ink you used, but when you first begin creating text or graphic elements, Director sets the ink to Copy.

Next, we'll change the ink style from Copy to Matte and then later to Bkgnd Transparent, so you can see the effect that these have on your finished animation.

Changing the Ink Style

Changing Ink styles is the easiest thing you'll do in Director. It's really about as simple as select, pull down, and redo your animation.

First, try changing the ink style of your text element to Matte. Then watch what happens as the text element crosses your video.

1. Select all the frames in the channel containing the text element. To do this, find the channel you used for your "Eggplant Parmigiana" and double-click on any frame with the Cast number in it.

2. Set the Ink style to Matte. To do this, pull down on the white panel at the left of the Score window, drag the mouse down to select Matte, and release.

3. Watch your movie! Press Command-1, Command-R, Command-P and see what happens. This time, the white space around the letters disappears when the text flies over the video. However, you can see that inside the closed letters g, p, and a the white background is still visible. To get rid of that, set the ink style to Bkgnd Transparent.

4. Make sure that all the frames in your "Eggplant Parmigiana" channel are selected. Look closely—if you haven't selected a different channel yet, Director has probably kept those frames highlighted. If they are not highlighted, select them all as described in step 1, above.

5. Set the Ink style to Bkgnd Transparent. As in step 2, pull down the Ink style menu and select Bkgnd Transparent from the list.

6. Watch your movie! Notice this time through how the trapped areas inside the closed letters are transparent—you can see the video through them as the letters crawl up the screen. When you add a background image to your Director title, that image will be visible through the spaces in your letters as well.

Animation: Seeing the Impossible

So far in this chapter, you've done some simple animations. You've moved video elements around on the screen and made a block of text "fly on" as a title. You've played with ways of making different layers visible in different ways. You've learned about the best way to synchronize sound with pictures, which is to keep it in a digital video file using QuickTime or AVI.

But what about more complex animation? You've done a little, by picking the beginning and ending frames for elements on the screen to move between and letting Director work out the details of the in-between screens. There's a lot more you can do with Director, though, if you're ready to start doing your own animation. There's so much more, in fact, that it takes up a chapter all for itself. So get ready to make some digital cartoons, make ducks talk and carrots dance, and have a great time. All it takes is a little imagination and the ability to see the impossible.

CHAPTER

4

Creating Animation with Director

The Five Types of Animation

The previous chapter included a number of exercises designed to show you some of the ways that Macromedia Director can let you incorporate audio and video clips into your document. You saw how to make text appear and move over video in the way titles or credits roll over visual elements in the credits of a movie. You've even worked a little with moving the video clips on the stage. The technique you used to move text and video frames around the stage demonstrated one of the kinds of animation you can create with Director. Although we worked with imported video and text in the last chapter, you can use these animation techniques and more to move any visual element around in Director's stage.

The Five Types of Animation

There are basically five kinds of animation that Director can use:

- *Imported animation,* that is itself the output of a separate program designed to produce a particular kind of animation (for example, 3-D animation in the form of QuickTime movies)

- *Path-based animation,* like that demonstrated in Chapter 3, in which you define the beginning and ending points of an object's motion and let Director create the intermediate frames

- *Real-time animation,* in which you drag an object on the screen and Director copies the motion you define

- *Cel-type animation,* in which you create the different "poses" of a character's motion and let Director create "flip books" from the frames you draw.

- *Fast-sprite animation,* in which you develop characters that take little memory and permit fast response to user input

These types of animation are all compatible with one another. In fact, you can use them in combination to achieve some exciting results in your titles and documents. This chapter includes some examples that you can duplicate to see how to make things move on screen without going to the trouble and expense of digitizing video. Also covered is a simple way to use sprites in a game-like format, in which characters hide behind objects on the screen as they move.

Using Imported Animation

Director lets you import any external animation as a sequence of images, the same way you brought in video clips in Chapter 3. For example, you might use a 3D modeling program to render realistic simulations, store the images in a series of individual frames, and display them one after the other as though they were animated movies. Movies of this kind include animation from external sources, including popular morph applications, flight simulators, and other special-purpose animation or simulation tools.

Recall the discussion in Chapter 3 about ink styles. One ink style in particular, Bkgnd Transparent, has an interesting application for importing QuickTime movies, particularly 3D animations. (The Matte ink style, which is so similar to Bkgnd Transparent, does not work with QuickTime movies.)

If you import a video clip with the ink set to Bkgnd Transparent you'll notice that bright highlights become invisible. For example, in the following picture, the gleams from the hood of the car disappear and let the image behind (in this case, a solid blue background) show through. In Figure 4.1 it's disturbing, but you can use this technique to your advantage if you plan carefully. You can use this method to achieve a "blue screen" or chroma-key effect. Chroma keying is the technique used in television to superimpose the weather reporter over the satellite photos; it's traditionally done on a blue (or sometimes green) background, but in professional video it can be done on any color. Here's the basic procedure:

1. Create your 3D animation on a white background. Using an outside animation program such as Macromedia's MacroModel, or an outside vendor's product such as Specular 3D, animate objects on a solid white background. Be sure not to use very bright highlights or white areas in your models, as they will also disappear after step 4. One trick is to change the colors of the lights you select in the 3D scene: Set the lights to a bright version of a color that will look natural in your setting, such as yellow for an exterior shot.

2. Save the animation as a QuickTime movie.

3. Import the QuickTime movie into Director.

4. Set the sprite to use the ink style Bkgnd Transparent.

Figure 4.1
Importing video clips with the ink set to Bkgnd Transparent causes bright highlights to disappear. Highlights drop out, but other colors remain.

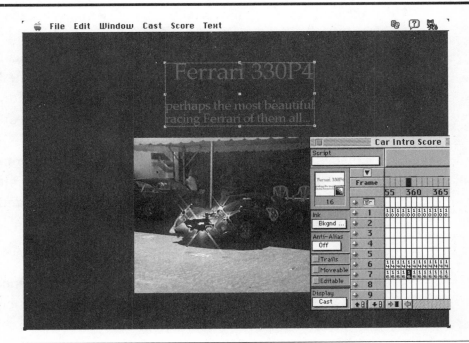

5. Make the entire QuickTime movie visible. To review, you make the movie visible by selecting all the frames of the movie, then selecting In-between Linear from the Score menu or typing Command-B. If you need more review, look at the exercises in Chapter 3.

6. Watch your movie!

By now the Command-1, Command-R, Command-P keyboard sequence should be second nature, as though you were playing a practiced tune on the piano. See how it looks—do the highlights work as you'd hoped? Do you need to modify the color in your 3D animation to work with Bkgnd Transparent ink in the way you want? Keep trying, and remember that because the color values are digital, you only need to change the color by one location in the color map to get it to appear or drop out. But you'll have to do that in the outside animation.

Animating Pieces of Imported Graphics

You can also use a graphics editor to cut elements out of an external program and use these in Director. For example, you can import a video frame or a digital picture into Adobe Photoshop, cut out part of that frame, save the cutout, and use it as your animated character. Fans of animator Terry Gilliam, who produced all the cutout animation in the Monty Python shows and movies over the years, know what cutout animation can do.

You can make your own digital cutout animation by opening a framegrabbed image (or any other image) in an image management tool like Adobe Photoshop or Aldus Photostyler and following these steps:

1. Select the Lasso tool.

2. If your screen is large enough or your image small enough, pull down the Window menu and select Zoom In. This increases the size of the image's pixels, making it easier for you to select the right part of the picture.

3. Hold down the mouse button and trace around the outline of the object you wish to make into a cutout.

4. When you have finished outlining the object, let up on the mouse. The outline of the object will flicker (sometimes called the "crawling ants" border), signifying that you have selected it.

5. Type Command-C (or Control-C in Windows) to copy the region to the Clipboard.

6. Pull down the File menu and select New. Photoshop for the Macintosh displays the dialog box shown in Figure 4.2.

7. To create a cutout for use in Director, be sure to select the White radio button, not the Background Color button, at the bottom of the dialog box. Then click OK. This opens a new, empty file the size of the smallest rectangle that can contain the image you cut out in steps 3, 4, and 5.

Figure 4.2
Photoshop's
New File
dialog box

```
┌──────────────────────── New ────────────────────────┐
│  ┌─ Image Size: 2K ──────────────────┐    ┌────────┐ │
│  │                                   │    │   OK   │ │
│  │    Width:  [23    ] [ pixels ▼]   │    └────────┘ │
│  │                                   │    ┌────────┐ │
│  │   Height:  [22    ] [ pixels ▼]   │    │ Cancel │ │
│  │                                   │    └────────┘ │
│  │ Resolution:[72    ] [pixels/inch ▼]             │ │
│  │                                   │              │ │
│  │     Mode:  [ RGB Color    ▼]      │              │ │
│  └───────────────────────────────────┘              │ │
│  ┌─ Contents ──────────────────────┐                │ │
│  │   ◉ White                        │                │ │
│  │   ○ Background Color             │                │ │
│  └──────────────────────────────────┘               │ │
└──────────────────────────────────────────────────────┘
```

8. Type Command-V (Control-V in Windows) to paste the pixels you copied in steps 3, 4, and 5 into the file you created in steps 6 and 7.

9. Save the file and note the name.

Following these steps will result in a file that contains the image you cropped from the full-scale screen, with no other image area outside it. Figure 4.3 shows the result of cutting an image of a Ferrari from a frame of video shot at a race track. (Ferraristi will no doubt realize that the file name is incorrect; this is of course a 275GTB, not a 250.)

You now have a file suitable for use in Director. When you clicked the White radio button to specify the background color, you made it possible using Director's Matte ink style to draw just the picture, without the background, on top of any images in a lower-numbered channel. Figure 4.3 illustrates how this might look, with the Ferrari (here with its correct name) superimposed over a sunset.

Figure 4.3
The only approved way to cut up a Ferrari

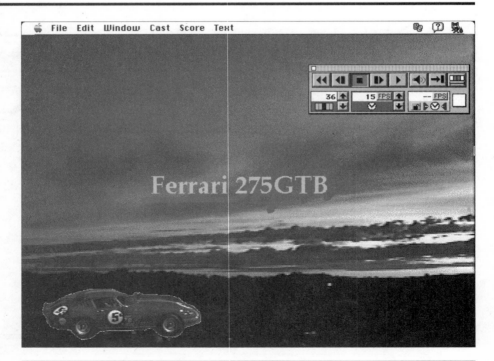

To use this procedure in Director, select an open Cast member window, then pull down the File menu and select Import. Use the file selection menu to find the file you saved out of Photoshop and import it into the open Cast member window. You can now use this image just as you can any image you created with Director's own Paint tool. You can also paint over it, retouch it, or otherwise manipulate it just as though you had created it in Director.

For our purposes, we're going to work on using imported images as well as custom-drawn images in animation. The next section describes how you might make the Ferrari race across the screen, perhaps in synchronization with a sound track.

Working with Path-based Animation

You've already done some path-based animation, both with text and with the video images in Chapter 3. In this chapter, we'll break the path up into smaller segments, showing how you can move a sprite all the way around the stage, making it bounce off the walls, change speed, and do a few other things.

The trick to doing this efficiently in Director is to remember that when Director "in-betweens" a sprite in a sequence of frames, you can pick up and leave off the sprite's motion seamlessly by clicking on an existing frame in the score as one end of a series of frames that you want Director to interpolate for you. When you use Command-B to determine the in-between frames in the score, Director only calculates between the two frames you have selected.

For example, if you select frame 1 and frame 3, Director will interpolate only one frame, frame 2, when you type Command-B. Likewise, if you select frame 3 and then drag that cast member into frame 10 of the same channel, Director will only interpolate between frames 3 and 10 when you type Command-B. This lets you change the speed and direction of a sprite as it moves across the screen; if you move the same distance on the screen in three frames as you do in six, the sprite will move half as fast in the six-frame sequence as it did in the three-frame sequence.

The previous technique is a good one for matching the motion of sprites on the screen to sound tracks or to one another, because you can position the sprite where you want it on a given frame. When you choose In-between Linear, Director interpolates an even amount of motion between each frame in the animation.

But not much in nature actually moves in this fashion. The method just described is a decent way to animate titles and text fly-ons, for instance, but not a good way to simulate the behavior of a moving car or a flying bird. For that, you want to change the rate dynamically—that is, have the object appear to accelerate or decelerate as it moves. One way you can do this is to choose progressively finer and finer resolution on the sequences you have Director interpolate, so that each frame represents a smaller and smaller motion. There's also a built-in way to change the speed of a path-based animation: Select the In-between Special option of the Score menu. After doing so Director will display the following dialog box:

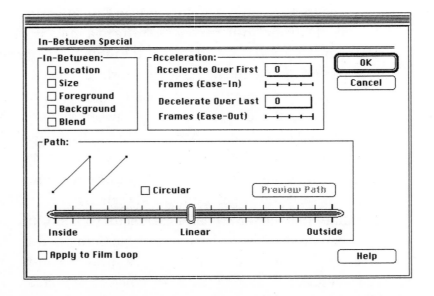

The Acceleration options let you change the rate at which your object moves, at the beginning or ending of its path. To use this feature, follow these steps:

1. Position your sprite at the first location along the path. To do this, drag the cast member into the Score window to select the channel and frame, then move the sprite on the stage until it is at the place where you wish it to begin.

2. Position your sprite at its final position along the path. Again, drag the cast member into the same channel, this time selecting the last frame in the sequence you wish to create.

3. Select all the frames between (and including) the first and last locations. To do this, click on either the first frame or the last frame, then use the horizontal scroll bar to display the other end of the sequence. When you see the other end, hold down the Shift key and click the mouse button on the frame.

4. From the Score menu, select In-between Special.

5. Choose the number of frames over which you wish the sprite to speed up or slow down. The shorter a number you select, the more rapid the acceleration or deceleration. To make something screech to a halt, choose 4; to make it glide gracefully to rest, choose 32.

6. Watch your movie!

In practice, linear interpolation is a good way to rough out your motion, determine where an object needs to be at a given frame, or provide instant changes in direction. For finer control, In-between Special lets you move objects in ways that look much more realistic for most kinds of motion.

Compound Paths: A Study in Interpolation

One place where you can see the difference between linear and special interpolation in the real world is on a billiard table. When you roll a cue ball across the surface of the table, it keeps a reasonably constant speed for most of its travel. Certainly when the ball bounces off the edge of the table, you can't see it slow down—it simply changes direction and appears to retain all of its velocity, at least until it starts slowing. Here's an exercise that gives you practice changing directions and speed in the same short clip. For now, you'll need two cast members: a circle (representing the cue ball) and a line (representing the edge of the table). As an alternative to the line, you can make a rectangle that effectively fills in the edge of the table, as shown in Figure 4.4.

Figure 4.4
The way the ball bounces (or at least what it bounces against)

Follow these steps to set the cue ball in motion.

1. Draw the line across the stage. To do this, you'll need to select an open Cast window; click Command-5 to open a drawing window; and select the Line tool and hold down the Shift key to draw a line straight across the window. Then drag the line into the Score window and place it in the first frame of channel 1. When it appears in the stage, drag it to the position you want it to take.

2. Make the line visible throughout your animation. The surest way to achieve this is to select frame 1, where you've drawn the line across the stage, and type Command-C. This copies the sprite in its location on the stage. Then choose an ending frame number—for this example, choose frame 120 to make an eight-second animation. Click on frame 120 of channel 1 and type Command-V. This pastes the sprite for the line into the same location in frame 120 as it was in frame 1. Then select frame 1 and frame 120 and type Command-B, or pull down the Score menu and select In-between Linear.

3. Draw a billiard ball. Select an unused Cast window and type Command-5 to open a drawing window; select the Ellipse tool and hold down the Shift key while drawing to make a circle.

4. Put the ball into the first frame of the animation. To do this, drag the ball from the Cast window into frame 1 of channel 2.

5. Drag the billiard ball to the lower left-hand corner of the stage. When you drag the ball into the frame, it appears in the middle by default. Drag it down to the lower left-hand corner of the stage so that its box aligns with the corners of the stage. Figure 4.5 shows an example.

6. "Roll" the ball up to the line across the stage. To do this, drag the ball into a suitable frame in channel 1—for example, frame 30

Figure 4.5
Aligning the
ball with the
corners of the
stage

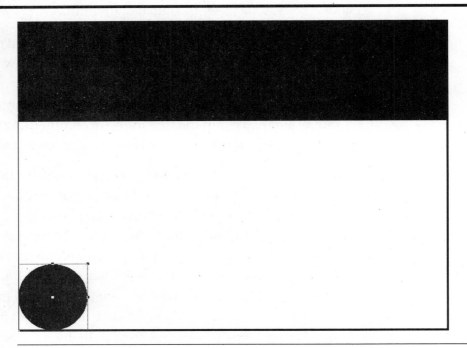

represents two seconds of animation. Then drag the sprite on the stage until its top lines up with the bottom edge of the "table."

7. Use In-between Linear to fill in the frames. Select frame 1, move the scroll bar to display frame 30, then Shift-Click to select all the intermediate frames. Then type Command-B to fill in the frames between 1 and 30.

8. "Roll" the ball to the lower right corner. Move the ball from the Cast window into frame 60 of channel 1; this will position the ball at that location after two seconds. When the sprite appears on the stage, drag it into the lower-right corner of the stage so that the lines of the sprite line up with the edges of the stage window.

9. Animate the roll with a slow deceleration. To make the ball roll slowly to a stop, select frame 30, Shift-Click on frame 60, then go to the Score menu and select In-between Special. Leave the

Accelerate Over First Frames field set to 0, and set the Decelerate Over Last Frames to 32, so that the ball slows gradually over the entire duration of its roll.

10. Leave the ball in its place for several seconds. Use a linear interpolation, and copy (Command-C) the ball from its final position at frame 60. Paste it into the same location (Command-V) in the final frame of your script, frame 120.

11. Watch your movie! Clear the screen (Command-1), rewind to the beginning (Command-R), and play (Command-P).

Now, critique the motion. You will probably notice that the ball takes too long to roll upwards; using the same duration for the roll up the stage as for rolling to a stop doesn't look right. So here's a suggestion: Make the ball hold still for the first 15 frames by pasting from frame 1 into frame 15 and doing a linear interpolation, then make the ball move from frame 15 to its location in frame 30, also using a linear interpolation. To recalculate, click on frame 15, then Shift-Click on frame 30 and type Command-B. The animation looks much more realistic with this simple change.

Using Real-time Animation

Path-based animation is a great technique for making titles fly onto a video image, graphics glide smoothly across a screen, or other visual elements move in straight lines from one place to the next. You can even combine several segments of path-based animation to make objects bounce, reflect, or veer sharply from one side to another.

Real-time animation also lets you take a sprite and trace its path around the screen, drawing it freehand, if you will. There are several things to remember about this:

■ If you move the mouse slowly or in a jumpy fashion, you can smooth out much of the motion by recording at a slower rate than you play back. For example, you can record at 15 fps and play back at 30 fps and the motion will look much smoother.

■ Director doesn't let you choose the channel in which you wish to animate your sprite this way; it automatically selects the next available channel. You can move the frames to another channel later if you choose (described later in this chapter).

■ Director begins to capture your mouse movements as soon as you press and hold the Control and Spacebar keys at the same time, then press and hold the mouse button. This does not begin a capture mode that you turn off later; the mode continues only as long as you hold down the Control key, the Spacebar, and the mouse button. If you let up on the mouse button or either of those keys before you are finished with your animation, Director stops recording.

■ Although you will need to see both the Score and the Cast windows as you set up for real-time animation, you can move them out of the way in order to watch where you move your sprite while Director is recording the animation. If you don't move them out of the way, Director will still capture the path you describe with your mouse while animating this way; you simply will not see the character when it goes under any of Director's windows.

The technique for doing real-time animation is simple:

1. Select the frame in which you want the animation to begin. To select the frame, click inside the box above the line containing the frame numbers—not in the cell inside the Score window. Director automatically animates into the next available channel; if you want to move the animation later, read the section, "Moving a Sequence of Frames" later in this chapter.

2. Select the cast member you want to animate. Don't drag it onto the stage—simply select it by clicking on the Cast window in which that cast member is stored.

3. Position the cursor where you want to begin your animation. Director will begin real-time animation, recording the path you draw, as soon as you perform the next step, so prepare by moving the mouse, allowing enough room on your desk for smooth, fluid motions, and otherwise make ready. You may wish to practice moving the cursor without capturing the animation; if so, you may need to repeat steps 1 and 2 if either the cast member or the beginning frame becomes deselected. When you're ready to begin, perform the next step.

4. Press and hold the Control key and the Spacebar, then hold the mouse button down and drag the mouse along the path you want your sprite to pursue. Drag the mouse smoothly; Director records every wiggle, bobble, or other singularity in the path you draw. Remember that recording at a slower speed than your title will play back can have a beneficial effect on the smoothness at run time.

5. When your sprite reaches the final location on its path, lift off the mouse, Control key, and the Spacebar. This stops recording. Director will store the frames in the next available channel. (One nice touch: If you have filled channel 1 with a background image that spans a fixed number of frames, and your real-time animation takes longer than that number, Director automatically extends the background image for the duration of the real-time animation.)

6. Watch your movie! It's important to check the appearance of real-time animations, because so many things can jump out at you afterwards that weren't apparent when you were concentrating on drawing the path.

If for some reason you don't like your animation—if there's a jump, a hiccup, a slow section, or some other problem—type Command-Z and Director discards the current real-time animation.

Modifying Sprites

If you modify the sprite after storing the real-time animation, Director uses the new version of the sprite in every frame. For example, you can use a dummy version of a character or an icon—something as simple as a box or a circle—to rough out the motion. Then, as your art department refines the appearance of the character, you can plug the new art into the cast member that you've animated, and Director will update the entire animation with the new character.

Additionally, this means you can copy complex paths into new documents, change the appearance of the cast member that's taking this path through the screen, replace the background elements, and you will have a completely new animation based on the same motion as your first animation—without having to replace all the intermediate frames. For instance, if you are animating a chase between two characters, you can have the villain running through the forest in one scene, then copy the whole document, replace the villain's cast member with art of the hero, and show the hero hot on the heels of the evildoer, avoiding the same trees and the same stones in the same forest scene. (Later on, when we discuss synchronizing events in Chapter 6, we'll look at how you can "splice" two separate Director files into a single movie.)

Moving a Sequence of Frames

There are several reasons you may want to move a sequence of frames from one part of the score to another. You may want to move a sequence earlier or later in the animation, or you may want to move a sequence into another channel. For example, when you use real-time animation, Director automatically stores the animation frames in the first available channel. This can cause effects you may not be expecting, because of the way Director indicates which objects appear in front and which objects appear behind in a given scene.

Following these steps will move a sequence of frames from one channel into another. The result will be to move the frames closer to the "audience."

1. Determine the sequence you need to move. To do this, watch your animation and pay attention to the playback head to see where the sequence in question begins and ends. You can also single-step the playback head, either by clicking the frame forward button on the Control window or simply by dragging the mouse to the left and right in the Score window.

2. Select the first frame in the sequence you want to move. To do this, use the horizontal scroll bar until the first frame appears in the Score window.

3. Select the last frame in the sequence and Shift-Click. This selects the entire sequence between the two end points you chose in step 2 and step 3.

4. Cut the frames, saving them onto the clipboard. To do this, type Command-X when the frames you want are highlighted. The frames disappear from that channel in the Score window.

5. Select a new location and paste the frames there. To do this, click on the frame and channel where you want the sequence to start, then type Command-V. For example, to move a sequence of frames out from behind a background illustration, paste the sequence into any channel with a number that is higher (closer to the bottom of the Score window) than the channel number used to contain the background illustration itself.

Fast Sprite Animation

If absolute blazing performance is your goal—if you're creating a fast-paced action game—your sprites should all be 1-bit graphics, and should all be animated with Matte ink. Here's why: An 8-bit sprite (that is, a sprite that uses 256 colors) takes up eight times as much memory and requires eight times as long to animate as a 1-bit sprite.

Does that mean the fastest sprites can be black and white only? Not at all. 1-bit sprites simply define two colors, a foreground and a background, and use a single bit (a 1 or a 0) to identify those two colors in memory. The key is that you need to set the foreground and background colors for the sprite, not for the cast member; but you have to set the cast member to 1-bit before you can meaningfully set foreground and background colors for the sprite.

Here's the procedure:

1. Select the cast member from the Cast window. You can select more than one cast member at a time by holding down the Shift key when you click on each subsequent pane in the Cast window.

2. Pull down the Cast menu and select Transform Bitmap. The Transform Bitmap dialog box appears; it contains a pull-down box titled Color Depth. From that, select 1 bit.

3. Choose Dither or Remap to closest colors. Dithering is a graphical technique that involves putting pixels near one another to give the illusion of more colors than the image can contain. (Much Impressionist painting, particularly the pointillist work of Georges Seurat, involves something much like dithering; essentially it involves letting the eye blend colors, rather than the canvas or the computer screen.) In black-and-white, a dithered image will look more like a coarse half-tone image in print. Remapping to closest colors, on the other hand, creates an image in which the individual colors are much more solid.

Figure 4.6 shows an image printed in its original 256 grays, then the same image converted to 1-bit art with Dither set and to 1-bit art with Remap to closest colors set.

4. Click OK. Director warns you that it cannot undo a change to a cast member's depth; you may wish to try the dithering and remapping of colors on copies of the cast member, rather than on the cast member itself.

Now the cast member is ready to create a fast, 1-bit sprite. By default, all 1-bit graphics are black and white, and you may find that adequate for the character you're designing. However, you can change the colors to any two in the palette, with the following technique:

I. Select the frames in which the cast member appears. Do not select the cast member itself; remember, you're working with the sprite, not the cast member. To select all the frames, click on the first frame in the sequence, then scroll to display the last frame

Figure 4.6
256 grays, dithering, and remapping

in the sequence; hold down the Shift key and click the last frame, and Director selects all the frames between the two end points.

2. From the Window menu, pull down and select Tools. Director displays the Tools window:

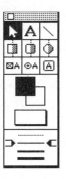

3. Select a foreground and a background color. When you hold the mouse button down over the squares representing the fore-ground and background colors in the Tools window, Director pops up a palette of available colors. Choose two colors for your sprite that work in the design scheme you have for your title.

Animating Frame by Frame

The final type of animation discussed here is frame by frame animation, similar to traditional cel animation. In either, you need to learn to think in small increments, seeing the short discrete steps that give the illusion of fluid motion. Frame-by-frame animation is a compli-cated craft that's difficult to learn, but Director simplifies what had been the most time-consuming part of it for many years: playing back your animation after you've designed it. Still, creating really good animation is an art that can take years to master.

We'll start with a very simple demonstration, a pair of butterfly wings flapping. Figure 4.7 shows the frames.

Figure 4.7
Flying
butterfly wings
as a sequence
of frames

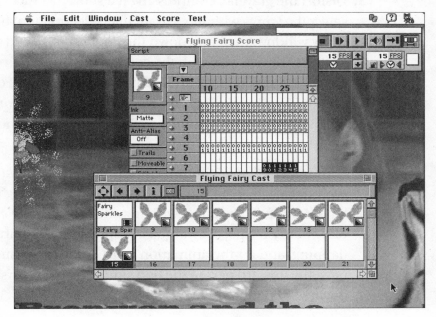

Follow these steps to create the frames that appear above:

1. Draw the wings in cast member 9. To open the Draw window, type Command-5 with cast member 9 selected, then select the draw tools you wish to use to create your art.

2. Copy the wings from member 9 to member 10. To do this, select the region of the Cast drawing window that contains the wings with the rectangular selection tool and type Command-C to copy. Then select cast member 10, type Command-5 to open the Draw window, and type Command-V to paste the wings in. Here's one of the neatest things about Director: It automatically pastes your art in the same location in each window. You don't have to do anything special to get the figures to line up in the stage. The first time I did this, I was impressed at how thoroughly the program simply "does the right thing," and I'm still impressed.

3. Distort the graphic, compressing it a short distance. To do this, select the wings with the rectangular selection tool from the Draw window, then pull down the Effects menu and select Distort. This lets you grab the corners of the region you have selected and pull them individually in any direction. For this animation, I pulled the top corners down and the bottom corners up, but not in even amounts so that it would look more like each wing was moving at its own pace.

4. Repeat steps 2 and 3 until the wings are at the lowest point of their flap cycle. I did this by eye; if you are modeling realistic behavior carefully, you may wish to watch them more closely than I did. For my purpose, I wanted a looping cycle of butterfly wings flapping, and for the animation I was doing it was sufficient to have the upward part of the flap simply be the reverse of the downward part, as follows.

5. Copy the graphics from each cast member, in reverse order, into the subsequent frames.

In Figure 4.7, you can see that the frames from 9 through 12 are the downward part of the butterfly's flap; frame 13 is copied from 11, frame 14 is copied from 10, and frame 15 is copied from frame 9. Now, how can you see the wings flap?

1. Choose a beginning frame in an empty channel, and drag cast member 9 into it. This puts a sprite of the butterfly wings onto the stage.

2. In the next frame of the same channel, drag cast member 10. This puts the second sprite of the flap cycle into the next frame of the movie.

3. Repeat step 2 for cast members 11 through 15. This puts one complete flap cycle into the picture.

4. Watch your movie!

If you have used the middle of another Director document, you may wish to select only the frames that include your butterfly animation. To do this, pull down the Edit menu, select Selected Frames Only, and then play your animation.

Flapping wings provide a special case in animation, but one that you may encounter again and again: the film loop. There's one trick to making a film loop look realistic: You'll want to drop cast member 15 from the loop, because it duplicates cast member 9. If you animate members 9 through 15 as a single loop, there'll be a pause at the top of every flap as the butterfly essentially holds its wings for an additional frame. So if you plan to loop animation, remember to stop one frame short of completing the cycle because that frame will be included on the next cycle of the loop.

C H A P T E R

5

Text: More Than Another Kind of Bitmap

Pictures, sound, and motion provide a real sense of computer multimedia, and are probably the flashiest ways to get someone's attention. So far, you've seen ways to bring several kinds of media into your Director movie. You've seen how to manipulate video clips as a component of your title and use QuickTime to synchronize sound to motion in the most reliable way possible. You've also seen how to animate objects on the screen, such as moving a video window, titles, or even buttons. But another medium exists on the computer: text.

Text is largely ineffective in movies or television due to the inflexible time element of film and video. The basic problem is that while everyone sees at the same speed, not everyone reads at the same speed. And since reading comprises two distinct components—decoding and comprehension—movies and television are limited in how much information they can display in text form. Two familiar examples of text as a medium on the computer are the credits that roll up at the end of movies, and the highlights or reviews of the steps covered in the video segment of popular how-to shows. This chapter discusses how to use text in Director, but more importantly it covers when and why text is the right medium for presenting a particular piece of information.

Adding Text to Director Movies

You can add text to your Director movies in either of two ways:

- As bitmaps, in which the text is an integral part of drawings, animations, and other visual elements

- As pure text, which can scroll, wrap to the size of the window you specify for it, and is much easier to edit or revise the content

In order to determine which approach you want to use, try answering the following question: Do you want to use text as a visual medium or do you want to use text for its message? The following discussions will serve as a useful guideline for making this decision.

Text as Medium

The first way you can add text into a Director movie is to use it as a visual element, the way you'd use a drawing, photograph, or sequence of video. Some of the reasons you might include this kind of text are

- Titles—both the overall title of your movie and any section headings, screen titles, or other information that comes up during play

- Captions—under figures, illustrations, or video sequences, for instance giving the name and title of the person speaking in a corporate video presentation adapted to Director

- Callouts—the names of components of a diagram for educational and training documents, countries on a map, components of a flowchart, and the like

- Buttons—the user interface for your title, letting you guide the user to other portions of your document

- Bullets—those short, just-the-facts pieces of text that make up slide show presentations

One way of distinguishing this kind of text from any other is to think of it as something you would paint on a sign: Be concise and precise. The text should be brief, clear expressions that you could read while driving past. After all, in the context of motion that multimedia provides, that's very much like what your readers will do.

In Director, you create such text with the same drawing tools you use for drawing animated characters, icons, and other visual elements. However, the Paint window is not suited for long pieces of text, for several reasons. Most notable among them is simply that editing text is somewhat laborious in the Paint window; you can erase what you typed while you are typing it, but you can't go back and re-edit the text once you move the mouse out of that region of text. Figure 5.1 shows the Paint window.

Figure 5.1
Director's
Paint window

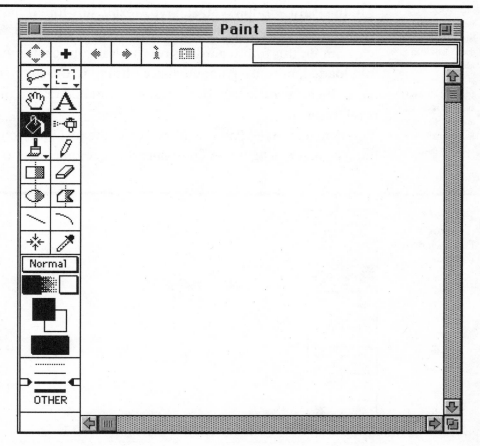

You may also be familiar with object editors, which let you select elements of an illustration such as rectangles, circles, lines, and strips of text, which you can then manipulate. Although Director doesn't include an object editor in its suite of capabilities, you can create illustrations in an object editor, such as Macromedia Freehand, and import them into the cast.

Director's Paint window is a bitmap editor like the familiar MacPaint program. When you let up on the mouse in a bitmap editor, whatever you have drawn or typed is there and you can't change it. (Text in HyperCard is the same way; if you put it in the drawing window of a card, it's there unless you erase the bitmap and retype it.) You can of course use the Command-Z keystroke to undo the last thing you did in Paint; if your hand slips on the mouse and you get an unintentional squiggle in a diagram, you can use Command-Z to erase it—though you'll lose that whole mouse stroke.

In the Paint window, you can type text in any font that exists on your workstation. Once you have typed it into a bitmap, your movie will contain this font regardless of whether your customers have that font loaded, because Paint creates a bitmap in the shape of each letter in the font you selected. It's just as if you had drawn them in, pixel by pixel.

To type text in the Paint window, select the text tool from the toolbar (see Figure 5.2). When you select the text tool, the cursor changes

Figure 5.2
Director's Paint window tool bar

Director's Text tool

to an I-bar. When you click on a region of the Paint window, Director boxes in a rectangle and gives you a flashing insertion point.

Your use of the Paint window will be more effective if you can develop the habit of selecting your font, size, and style before you start typing. In practice, Director lets you change the font, size, and style any time before you click the mouse again outside the region of text you are drawing. However, one advantage to selecting the font first is that you will see the text in its full, finished size. Furthermore, once you click the mouse to do some other operation, that text is added to the screen with its font, size, and style fixed.

Drawing Underneath Existing Text

To superimpose text on a colored background, you can type the text, select it with the lasso, and then drag it onto the colored region that represents the background of your title, button, or other graphical element. You will, however, have to use the Fill tool (that's the bucket) to add the background color to the trapped areas inside the letters (the middle of letters such as O, g, P, B, and the like). But painting *under* the existing patterns is more than just fun to watch. It lets you set the type, highlight it with contrasting colors, and add design elements to various parts of the text.

It's much easier to fit the graphic to the text when you know the size and color of the text. In Figure 5.3, the text came first, then the squiggle was written later but made to appear beneath the text. In Director, this drawing technique involves using the Switch ink.

To use the Switch ink, follow these steps.

1. Type in the text you want. Again, it's easiest if you select the font, size, and style you like before you begin typing. That way you won't accidentally click the mouse outside the region you're typing and have to restart later to get the correct font, size, or style.

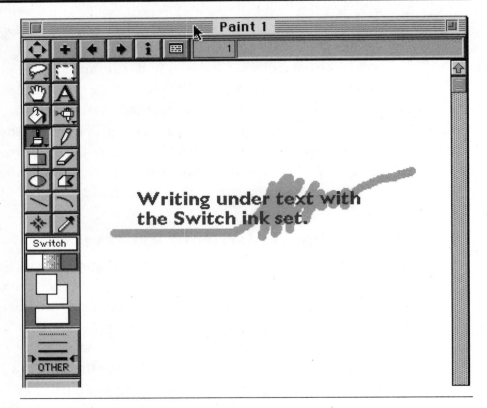

Figure 5.3
Effect of using
the Switch ink
in Paint

2. Select the Eyedropper tool (see Figure 5.4) and choose the background color. The Eyedropper tool lets you pick up a color from the screen so that you don't have to worry about what slot in the color map you assigned to a color on the screen. For this exercise, choose the white background color behind the letters.

3. Select a destination color. Click and hold the mouse in the destination color chip, shown in Figure 5.5. When you hold the mouse button down, Director displays a color palette; choose the color you want to draw under the text.

4. Select the brush tool. You can also double-click on the brush in the toolbar to pop up a dialog box showing brush shapes, sizes, and types.

Figure 5.4
The Eyedropper tool

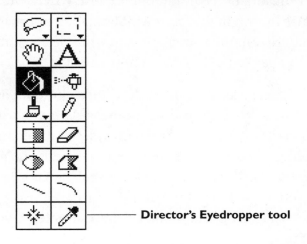

———— **Director's Eyedropper tool**

Figure 5.5
The destination color chip in the Paint toolbar

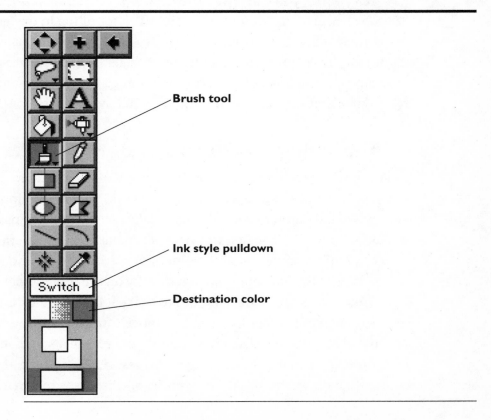

Brush tool

Ink style pulldown

Destination color

5. Draw the destination color under the text. When you hold down the mouse button in the Paint window, Director traces your motions underneath the text, filling it in with the current size, shape, and pattern of brush you have selected.

The Switch ink is useful for other drawing techniques as well. For instance, if you used a pen-and-ink drawing style, you can add tint to the white parts after you've drawn the lines of the composition, without having to worry about covering the lines. If you're used to painting or drawing on paper, Switch will feel backwards and rather exciting. If you're used to painting on the wrong side of a transparency—such as on an animation cel, for example—Switch will feel perfectly natural.

Of course, you can always fill in "top-layer" details with the pencil, the airbrush, or a different ink style. But for filling in designs behind text, Switch ink is a useful, fast way to achieve a little flash in your text buttons, titles, and credit lines. It's also a good way to apply some contrasting colors to text elements if they move or appear over a color that is too close to the color you have selected for the text.

Animating Words and Letters

Chapter 3 contains an exercise in which you move text over a video clip. That's one useful way to bring text into your animation. But there are several different ways you can make text come alive inside your Director movie. The first way involves making the text element you select follow some visual element in the scene; the second is by animating individual letters so that they fly on the screen one at a time.

You can shrink a text element to make it look smaller, and hence farther away, so that it appears to move toward the camera as you make it its normal size. (You should not enlarge a text element beyond its normal size, as its jagged edges will look worse; the section, "Antialiasing: Smoothing the Outlines," discusses this in a little more detail.) The next exercise shows how to create a movie whose motion follows the first and last frames that appear in Figure 5.6. In the animated scene, the text element moves down the road directly toward the viewer.

1. Make your text element with its background. To do this, follow the preceding exercise under the section, "Drawing Underneath Existing Text."

2. Drag the text element (with its associated graphic) into frame 1. This puts it into the desired frame and channel. Remember to put this into a channel that is closer to the bottom of the Score window than the channel that contains the background illustration.

3. Place the text in the middle of the road. By selecting frame 1 in the previous step, you automatically tell Director when the text element is to have the position and size that you give it in this step. If necessary, you can move the Score and Cast windows around on the screen to give you access to the right location on the stage.

4. Grab the text by one of its corner handles and shrink it. Move carefully, keeping the relative width and height roughly the same. Since this is only a short piece of animation and not a

Figure 5.6
A sample animation that shows how motion follows the illustrated frames

scientific simulation, you don't need to keep the relationship exactly correct in the shrunk version.

5. Choose a final frame for the animation. To determine this, decide how many seconds you want the animation to take, then multiply that number by 15 (or by your current frame rate if it is not 15 fps). If you want your animation to take two seconds, select frame 30. Use the horizontal scroll bar to view frame 30 in the Score window.

6. Drag the text element into the frame you selected in the previous step. As in step 2, dragging the text element from the Cast window into the frame in the Score window assures you of getting the cast member into the right time and place in your score.

7. Place the text element in the bottom corner at full size. As in step 3, move the Score and Cast windows if necessary to expose the lower left-hand corner of the stage, then drag the text element into a position between the edges of the roadway.

8. Calculate the intermediate frames with In-between Linear. To do this, select the first frame by clicking on it, then move to the last frame and hold down the Shift key while clicking on it. Then either pull down the Score menu and select In-between Linear, or type Command-B. This adds all the intermediate frames, calculating the change in size and in location for each stage of the process.

9. Watch your movie! To clear the stage, type Command-1. To rewind the movie to the beginning, type Command-R. To play it, type Command-P. You should see the text element move forward along the roadway, growing in size as it moves down and to the left. In the context of the perspective provided by the converging lines moving back into the forest, this clip gives the appearance of the text element moving toward the camera.

Another effect you can do easily with Director is to fly on the individual letters of a logo, a title, or some other element of your presentation. The following exercise shows you how you can do this using bitmapped text.

Creating Flying Letters

The trickiest part involved in making letters fly on one at a time is in making them line up properly once they're on the stage. This exercise shows you one way to line them up while you're developing your movie: draw a line in a separate cast member. That way you can place the letters in alignment on the stage, and when you're done you can simply remove the line from the score.

1. Create cast members for each of the letters. You can get as creative as you want here. You can use different styles, you can draw them by hand, you can make each letter an animated film loop as shown at the end of Chapter 4—you can do whatever you want to the appearance of the individual letters. Don't drag the letters into the score yet; leave them in the Cast window.

2. Create a cast member for the alignment mark on the stage. To do this, select an unused cast member in the window, pull up the Paint tool by typing Command-5, and draw a line that will be long enough to fit all the letters you want on a single line on the stage. Remember that holding down the Shift key while you draw the line will make the line snap to one of the quadrants, so if you want the letters to line up perfectly horizontally use the Shift key.

   As an additional trick, you can create markers along the length of this line to indicate where to place the letters if you want them evenly spaced. One way to do this is to create a separate element in the Paint window, one that has a fixed horizontal spacing and small vertical lines to indicate its end points. Then you can select this with the Lasso (not the Rectangle tool, which will pull in the surrounding background color) and drag it onto the overall alignment mark, giving you another cue for where to place your letters. This also works with other visual elements in your scene.

3. Place the alignment mark where and when you want it on the stage. To do this, drag it into the Score window in a channel closer to the bottom of the window than any other channel you intend to use. This way the other visual elements will all appear underneath it as you align them on the stage. Then make sure that the alignment mark is visible during all the frames within which you intend your letters to be animated. To do this, put it in the first and last frames in the scene, select both endpoints, and type Command-B to make Director calculate the in-between frames.

4. Determine the times at which you want each letter to fly on the stage. If you want them to fly on one at a time, pick separate frames for each letter to start, multiplying the portion of a second between each letter by your frame rate. (We'll talk more in the next chapter about synchronizing events.) Or if you simply want them all to fly on at the same time from different quadrants on the screen, determine when this fly-on is to begin. An alternative suggestion for this step is to work backwards: Decide when you want all the letters to appear together, choose that frame, and then calculate how far back in time you want them to make their first appearance. This can help you match your animation to an existing sound effect, for example.

5. Assign a separate channel to each letter in your cast. In the previous step, you determined the frame in which each letter would start (and possibly end) its animation. Now you need to assign each letter to its own channel in the Score window. Drag the cast member for each letter into the frame at which that letter's animation begins. You may find it easier to perform steps 5 and 6 together for each individual letter.

6. Align the letters on the stage in their initial locations. If you want the letters to appear to fly onto the screen from off-camera, drag them carefully by the border that appears when you select the frame in the Score window that contains them. It works most easily if you grab the letter initially by the edge of the border that is farthest from the direction in which you will be moving the letter. For example, if you want a letter to fly on stage from the viewer's left, grab the letter on the stage by its rightmost edge. When you have performed steps 5 and 6 for every letter in your animation, you're ready for the next step.

7. Align the letters together on the stage in their final arrangement. Place the letters where they will be when the entire word is visible. This is where you use the alignment mark you drew back in step 3. You may choose to align the tops of the letters or the bottoms. Note also that Director leaves the current frame selected (as indicated by the position of the playback head in the Score window). This helps you position all the letters as you want them to appear in the same frame.

    Tip: Save your movie frequently during this step. That way if you accidentally drag the background or some other element of your scene, you can recover easily. And remember that Command-Z will undo the last change you made, but only that one—once you move another cast member, the previous change becomes fixed.

8. Animate each channel individually, calculating the intermediate frames. To do this, click the beginning frame of each letter's fly-on, shift-click the end frame of the same letter's channel, and type Command-B. This makes Director calculate the intermediate frames for each letter's animation.

9. Remove the alignment bar from the Score window. To do this, double-click the channel in which you placed the alignment bar.

This selects all its frames. Then press the Delete key and the alignment bar's frames disappear from your scene.

10. Watch your movie! To clear the stage for display, type Command-1. To rewind the movie to the beginning, type Command-R. To play it, type Command-P.

Now you can fine-tune your animation. For example, if you followed the steps carefully, you'll notice that the letters disappear after they're in final position. There are several ways to make them stay visible; for now, just copy the last frame of each letter, one at a time, by selecting it and typing Command-C. Then move to the last frame in which you want the letters to remain visible and paste the frame you copied, typing Command-V. Then select the frames you just copied and pasted and use In-between Linear (Command-B) to fill them with the immobile image of the letter in that channel (Chapter 7 covers another way to do this).

As practice, try a short sequence in which the letters fly on one at a time but in order, as if being written by a typewriter. You can either leave the written letters in position (as on a modern electric typewriter), or you can leave the typing location fixed and move the other letters to the left (as on an old-fashioned manual typewriter). As a visual suggestion, especially for the old-fashioned typewriter approach, leave your letters two or three pixels up or down from the alignment bar.

Antialiasing: Smoothing the Outlines

You can smooth the outlines of text drawn in the Paint window by choosing a level of antialiasing from the Score window. Figure 5.7 shows where to find this.

Antialiasing smooths the edges of anything you create in the Paint window. This includes illustrations as well as text, though for the

Figure 5.7
The Anti-Alias pulldown in the Score window

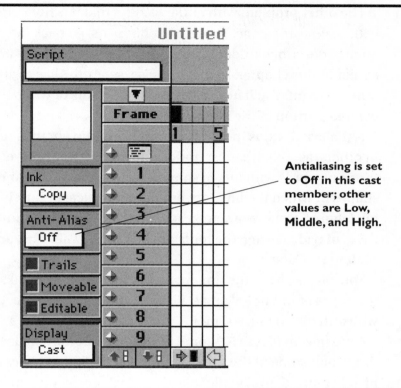

Antialiasing is set to **Off** in this cast member; other values are **Low, Middle,** and **High.**

sake of clarity I'll only mention text in this section. To perform antialiasing, Director blends the pixels at the edge of the text with the pixel underneath in the background. Then, when the text is drawn on the background, the edges appear softer and the stair-step effect, sometimes called "jaggies," diminishes.

There are a couple of problems with antialiasing. First, it is a tremendous user of processing power. Turning antialiasing on, even to a low level, will delay the display of a scene in which it's set. However, if you are saving your Director movies in QuickTime, there is no performance hit at playback, as Director calculates all the necessary pixel values when you export to QuickTime. This is one way to get smoothness and performance.

The other problem with antialiasing is that it is not compatible with scaling an image. To see what happens, go back into the sequence described under the section, "Animating Words and Letters," earlier in this chapter. In that exercise, set Anti-Alias to any value other than off. You'll notice flashes and flickers of white inside the colored portion of the illustration.

Antialiased text is more important in certain circumstances than in others, as well. It's most noticeable in fonts with curved letter forms or words with lots of smooth curves, diagonals, and other shapes in which the lines are not purely vertical or purely horizontal. Figure 5.8 shows a screen snapshot illustrating a number of cases of bad aliasing; the fonts are Black Oak, Gill Sans, and Monotype Corsiva.

You can see from the uppercase O's that the font breaks up around the edges of its curved areas. Figure 5.9 shows the same font, but with antialiasing set to High.

Note how in Figure 5.9 some of the detail in the smallest word drops out; some of the thinner curves of the italic O become completely blurred. And while these are black-and-white images, the blurring in color can have some unusual effects as the two pixel values from the foreground and the background are combined.

You must set the Ink style in the Score window to Matte or Bkgnd Transparent for antialiasing to show. If you leave the Ink style set to Copy, Director not only copies the text you see, but also the white "slug" that surrounds it.

Text as Message

So far, this chapter has shown you how to use text as a medium, as a way of painting signs that you use to point out areas of interest in your Director title. But there's more to text than saying "Wet Paint" or "This way to the egress." When considering any medium, it's hard not to think of Marshall McLuhan's well-known quote, "The medium is the message." What we do next will show you some ways to deconstruct this thought, to differentiate where the message itself—

Figure 5.8
Three fonts
that show
aliasing heavily

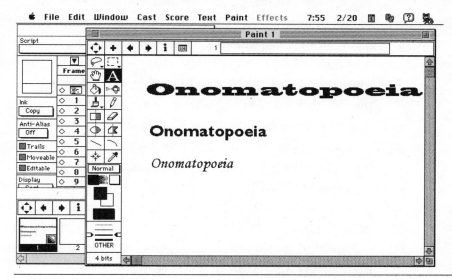

Figure 5.9
The same cast
member, but
with high
antialiasing

story, background, character, and motivation, as well as recitations of fact in nonfiction titles—is best served by the medium of text.

Consider these questions: When is text a message rather than a medium? How do you decide when text conveys information better than a graphical element with letters in it? How can you distinguish text as story rather than text as picture? And when is text the best way to convey information? Simply stated, there are times and circumstances when you need the clarity, precision, and density of information transfer that only text can provide.

This section will provide answers by establishing some rules about when to use text to convey messages in place of narration, video, or animation.

The static quality of text presents an advantage over moving media. Text on a computer screen keeps conveying its information until the user does something—turns the page, selects an option, or shuts off the computer. For example, a screen of text that contains instructions will remain visible for an indeterminate period of time. Your audience can reread text and click the Next page button when it's ready to move on. On the other hand, video instructions run once. Then you must either start from the beginning or move on to another sequence and if you miss this display, the information is gone.

Fitting the Text into a Moving Presentation

Where does text fit into a moving presentation? If you are designing a linear QuickTime movie that will run through once, the best use of text in the traditional linear form is certainly the back-story crawl at the beginning of *Star Wars*. George Lucas took an idea that had been around since the days of silent film. He put background information at the beginning, in text form, and let the audience read the setting for the dramatic action. In doing so, he also addressed the chief problem of adapting static text to a moving medium: Everyone in

the audience reads at a different rate. In the old days, fast readers were finished with the explanatory text several times before the film moved on, while slower readers might not finish the screen and might miss a point of plot development.

Lucas stepped outside the box and gave us text that moved at a well-chosen rate. It crawled up off the top of the screen fast enough to satisfy the quick readers in the audience—it gave them something to look at and wonder over while waiting for the next line to pop up. But it also moved slowly enough for the slower readers to finish it before it disappeared into the distance altogether.

Choosing the Right Display Rate   Human factors research points to the following data to help you determine the right rate for displaying text in your own documents:

- Create lines of text that are between three and seven words per line

- Choose a crawl rate that leaves each line on the screen for about 30 seconds altogether

Those two magic formulas—three to seven words per line, and a 30-second crawl rate—are the buffer size of the human short-term memory. That is, we can hold between three and seven pieces of information (words, in this case) in our memory for about 30 seconds at a time. Some people can do more, but few people can do less, so it's a good, safe value to choose for information transfer rate.

Creating a Scrolling Text Window

You can of course make text move with Director; we've done several such examples of this already. But if you're going to present more than a few words of text in one piece, you can leave text on the screen and let the user control how much of it remains up, and for how long. One way to accomplish this is by using the scrolling windows in Director's Text window. Scrolling windows allow you to add text to a window in your Director movie, even if the text itself extends beyond the limits of the window. A scrolling window then provides up and down arrows and an elevator bar that lets your audience scan the text for information. Here's how it works.

Like the Paint window, the Text window is bound to cast members. To create one, follow these steps.

1. Choose an unused cast member.

2. Pull down the Window menu and select Text Window. Alternatively, you can press Command-6 after selecting the cast member you wish to use for the Text window. Director pops up the Text window, with a number in the title bar that corresponds to the cast member you selected.

3. Add the desired text to the window. One advantage to using the Text window for text entry is that it contains a simple editor that lets you cut, paste, add, and delete text. You can also change the font, size, and style of individual words within the window. Director's Text window gives you most of the features of the SimpleText program for manipulating words and numbers. Figure 5.10 shows a sample Text window in Director. In addition to typing the text directly to the window, you can bring in text from other sources by cutting and pasting from the Clipboard or the Scrapbook. This works most easily if you have sufficient memory to run both the text program and Director at the same time; then it's simply a matter of going back and forth from one program to the next through the Application menu (the icon at the top right corner of the screen) on the Macintosh, or by the Task Switcher on Windows.

4. Click the information button on the text window. This displays the dialog box shown in Figure 5.11. From the selection box marked Style, choose Scrolling, then click OK.

Figure 5.10
A Text
window
associated
with cast
member 1

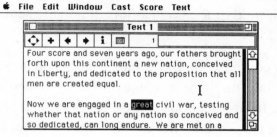

Figure 5.11
The Text Cast
Member Info
dialog box

5. Drag the cast member into the Score. This allows you to place it in the desired time as well as location in the sequence you are creating.

As a final comment on the opening scenes of *Star Wars*, you can make text crawl up the screen like the narrative text at the beginning of that film. In step 4, choose Adjust to Fit instead of Scrolling, then animate the text element just as you have the other kinds of text: position it at the starting frame, the ending frame, the appropriate positions of each on the screen, and then let Director generate the in-between frames.

In addition, you can use one text cast member as the repository of the overall text of the story, then cut from that cast member to make individual or partial cast members for use in other portions of your document. For example, the piece on *The Gettysburg Address* that I've used for the screen snapshots here might be developed into a document in which individual phrases taken from the address were used to highlight commentary from historians, illustrations of the cemetery, and other information from other media that you bring into the document to support, to illustrate, and to enlighten.

Text as Magic

In a world of 3D computer-synthesized velociraptors terrorizing a couple of children in an empty kitchen, of blood-spattered chainsaws and jack-in-the-box horror movies, of virtual reality and kids seeing 10,000 murders on television by the time they reach adulthood, it's easy to scorn the thought that text can be magical. It's just letters, after all, letters that people have to read, have to understand, have to work over before they get anything out of it. That's all true. But consider this: There's a very good, sound reason why in English at least, we use the same word to describe weaving a sequence of letters as we do to describe the weaving of magic. That word, of course, is "spell."

There is a particular part of human consciousness that is only accessible to, and by, text. For example, can you think of a way to convey the meaning of "Once upon a time" without using words? I won't state categorically that it can't be done. There are probably artists brilliant enough to convey that message in images, in ways that don't use text. But I've never met one.

Why and How Text Is Magical

Visual media address visual cognition, while text engages a different part of human consciousness altogether. Reading requires moving images out of the purely visual processing centers of the brain into the language center, on the left side of the brain above the ear. While reading becomes automatic it can never become unconscious the way recognition of visual elements in the optical processing centers of the brain becomes unconscious. For this reason I say that movies happen in the eyes, but books happen in the imagination. This complex transformation that takes place in our brains is partially responsible for the magical nature of text.

The final exercise in this chapter is designed to help you think about the most powerful, direct, and effective ways of using text to tap into the imagination. Then bring that same power into your other media.

I. Find one of the following pieces of music:

- "Pictures at an Exhibition" by Modest Mussorgsky (in particular the final two sections)
- "The Moldau" by Friedrich Smetana
- "Romeo and Juliet" by Peter Ilyich Tschaikovsky
- "The Russian Easter Overture" by Nikolai Rimsky-Korsakov

Your local public library may be a good source if you don't own any of these pieces.

2. Find a notebook and a pen or pencil to take notes; the more notes you make, the more you'll benefit from this exercise.

3. Relax, dim the lights, and put on the music you've selected. Don't dim the lights so much that you fall asleep; you'll need enough light to take notes, but try to eliminate all other distractions. You can do this exercise with a friend, family member, classmate, or colleague, but keep focused on the exercise.

4. As the music plays, let your mind focus on the images it suggests. What comes to mind when you hear the crashing of the brass in the next-to-last movement of "Pictures"? What images arise from the quiet, almost rippling opening theme of "The Moldau"? Let your imagination go; get in touch with your memories, your dreams, your own storehouse of images.

5. When an image appears, write it down. Don't sketch it. Don't draw it. Write it, in the clearest and most precise words you can. Write words that touch a sense other than vision, where possible. Choose tactile words, sharp as broken seashells on bare feet. Or choose auditory words, blaring garishly, screeching in terror, or cooing soothingly like a purring cat. But focus on making the transformation from music into the imagination by addressing some other sense, using the words that you write down on your notebook.

How will this exercise help your multimedia title development? The answer should be easy now. After all, if you can imagine powerful sensory words by listening to music, you should be able to imagine ways to apply that power to your multimedia projects.

The next chapter describes some strategies for adding sound, positioning the various elements of your movie along the time line, and for adjusting and manipulating the tempo of your finished movie. After that, it covers ways to apply interactivity to the elements you are designing.

CHAPTER

Synchronizing Events: The Director's Cut

What Happens When?

Creating Pseudo-Animations with Transitions

Endnote on Synchronizing Sound and Motion

When your layouts take on the added dimensions of motion and interactivity, you need to think about them differently. Controlling the pace, timing, and flow of your document in time is comparable to controlling the pace and flow of a static document such as a story, an article, a training or user's guide or a brochure—not to mention the pace and timing of a video or film presentation. Perhaps you've taken classes in video or filmmaking and learned to use cuts to pace your scenes, or in creative writing you probably learned to keep the pace dynamic by showing action rather than just telling about it—such skills from these other media apply directly to multimedia.

This chapter contains three main sections. It covers some strategies for rough synchronization to get your characters to interact in a way that's pretty close to what you want. These strategies represent the easiest way to get the basic flow, motion, and timing down so that you can see whether you want to proceed. You'll also read about some ways you can fine-tune the basic flow that you've developed using the strategies in the first part of the chapter. These include frame-by-frame tweaking of position, size, and other relationships between cast members.

The final section of this chapter introduces a new part of the Score window that I haven't talked about yet: the Tempo channel. This last section includes some exercises on how to slow down your play to keep synchronization intact on less powerful processors, how to make your movie wait for a video or audio segment to finish playing, and how to pause in a frame until the user clicks the mouse button.

Let's start with an examination of how to think about synchronization in the early stages of your movie's development.

What Happens When?

All moving media have a baseline from which they draw their tempo, their rhythm, their sense of synchronization. In music it's the drums; in movies it's often the score or sound track; in text it's the pace and pattern of sentences. Your work with animation in particular and Director in general will go much more smoothly if you think about your scenes as having some kind of visual "back beat" that provides the basic structure of the scene. But how can you identify it? It may well be the sound track; if you're working to synchronize events with an existing sound track, you can time the sound's play and use this as a way of determining the frames in the score in which your various cast members have their exits and their entrances. On the other hand, it may just as easily be a particular visual motion, such as an image sweeping across the field of vision or a character dancing across the stage.

Examine the scene and you should find that there is one motion, one element, one character that triggers the other motions. If there isn't, think harder about the scene; you probably want such a key character for dramatic reasons. Its usefulness in developing your Director presentation is strictly a side effect. Those of us who learned expository prose the old-fashioned way might consider this the visual "topic sentence" of the paragraph, or scene, that we're developing. And just as with the topic sentence, it's easiest if you animate this motion first because the other motions in the scene will support, enhance, or embellish the action you have identified.

Here are some questions you can ask to help determine this primary dramatic action:

■ What action initiates the other actions in the scene? In the example I'll talk about in several places in this chapter, it's a cat stalking and jumping after a bird. That's the trigger motion, the visual topic sentence, of the piece; the bird's flight is in direct reaction to, and a dramatic result of, the cat's stalking and pouncing. In short, it's the stimulus; the rest of the actions are one or another kind of response.

■ What action is at the center of the scene, dramatically or visually? It may not be the action that initiates the scene; it may occur later in the scene, or throughout the scene, without having any actions that are direct results of the first one (as the bird's flight is the result of the cat's stalking). A raft traveling downstream isn't the cause of the scenery changing, but it's the key to our perception of the shift in background.

■ What action provides dramatic background for which the other elements in the scene provide fulfillment? Comics talk about jokes and even whole routines as having setups and punch lines; you may not be doing a comedy title, but thinking of each scene in terms of setup and punch line will help you decide what to animate first.

The reason you animate the punch line, topic sentence, or dramatic center before animating anything else in that scene is to more easily facilitate hanging the rest of the scene's motion off the strong spine that the dramatic center provides. Once you see the stimulus, you can more easily determine when and where the responses will occur. Again, the decision of when to animate a particular dramatic action or character motion is really an issue of dramatic and thematic development; the fact that animating your main dramatic action first makes it easier to animate is a side effect of making it easier for you to visualize what the scene is about.

From a practical standpoint, there's another way of identifying what you may want to animate first. Chapter 4 discussed real-time animation, in which you hold down the Control key and the Spacebar while using the mouse to draw the path you want a cast member to take. If you want one of your characters to take a complex path that's a good sign that you should do the animation first, for a number of reasons. The most important reason is it will be more effective to structure other characters' motions in the scene around the real-time animation if that animation is already present. Once you have the real-time animation (which is likely to be the most complicated action in the scene anyway) in the score, you can step through your scene to determine where the character for which you drew the real-time animation is when you bring in other characters to respond to the main dramatic action.

Here's another significant reason to do the animation first. Once you have captured the basic frames from real-time animation, it is relatively easy to nudge the characters, change their speed, or otherwise manipulate them. This technique constitutes the least laborious way to work.

The Hunter and the Hunted

The clearest way to visualize action and reaction in a scene is to think of two characters in conflict. I live in a house filled with cats, so we regularly watch a supremely primal conflict as our cats try to catch birds in the backyard. It's the perfect way to demonstrate how one character's action (the cat's stalk and pounce) leads to another character reaction (the bird's flight to safety).

The animation from which I've taken the following snapshots demonstrates this visually, and also demonstrates the benefits of structuring your scenes around the real-time animation first. I blocked out this scene by having the cat make its stalk and pounce, then placed the bird where it needed to be for the cat's jump to look realistic.

For the following exercise, you'll need two cast members—a cat and a bird. You're going to make a short cartoon in which the cat stalks the bird, jumps for it, but misses as the bird flies away and out of the scene.

What Happens When?

115

1. Load the cat and the bird into the cast. If necessary, draw a quick sketch of the two adversaries. Be sure there are individual cast members for each character, as they're going to be moving different directions at different times.

2. Block out the cat's movement. Use the mouse (now you see why I have the cat chase a bird in this scene) to trace the cat's path. Start from the edge of the screen, and practice drawing the cat's path and speed.

3. Use real-time animation to animate the cat's stalk and jump. To do this, select the frame in the Score window at which you want the animation to start. Select the cat's cast member—don't drag it to the score, just click on it. Then move the mouse where you want the scene to begin and hold down the Control key and the Spacebar for the duration of your animation. Finally, hold the mouse button down (or the left button on the PC mouse) while you draw the cat's movements on the screen. When you're finished with your animation, let go of the mouse button and Director stops capturing frames.

4. Decide where the bird should start to fly away. There are several ways you can do this. The easiest is to select a frame about where you think the bird should start its flight away from the cat; try one where the cat is about at the height of its jump. From here, select frames one at a time on either side until you see the point at which you want the bird to start its flight.

5. Place the bird at its "launch pad." Drag the bird into the frame you selected in step 4. Director puts the bird's sprite into the middle of the stage; drag it to the appropriate location, which is the spot at which the cat lands in its leap. (Don't worry, you'll make the bird fly away before the cat reaches that spot.) One tip: I've been known to stick a couple of Post-It notes on the monitor to indicate the corners of the rectangle where I wanted to drag a

cast member. It's the same as a human director using tape to tell an actor where to stand on stage.

6. Determine the frame in which the bird should fly off-stage. And here's why you did the cat first: The cat's jump serves as a reference for the rest of the motion in the scene. Because the cat, with its more complex animation, is already in the scene, you can cue the bird's more direct motion against the cat's position on the stage. For this step, make the bird fly off the stage about the time the cat lands. Once again, to determine this, select frames one by one to see when the cat lands. And as a special trick, make sure that there is at least one frame in the cat's animation after the bird has reached the uppermost point in its flight.

7. Place the bird in the desired frame. The reason you left at least one frame in the cat's animation after the bird reaches the top of the stage is so that the bird will appear to have flown out of the picture. If you put a pause at the end of your animation, the bird will appear to hang in the air. This will work if you want to put a tree branch up for the bird to sit on, but the sense of escape is heightened by having the bird appear to leave the stage.

8. Position the bird on the stage. Again, Director automatically puts the sprite in the middle of the stage when you drag a cast member into the Score window. Drag the bird's sprite to the corner of the stage (or wherever you want the bird to escape to).

9. Select the first and last frames of the bird's flight, then choose In-between Linear from the Score menu. To do this, click on the first frame of the bird's flight, then scroll to where you can see the last frame; hold down the Shift key and click the last frame. Director selects all the intermediate frames in the sequence. Then, pull down the Score menu and select In-between Linear. Alternatively, you can type Command-B. Director fills in (or interpolates) the intermediate frames in the bird's animation.

10. Watch your movie! Command-1 clears the stage, Command-R rewinds the movie to the beginning, and Command-P plays it.

Of course, there are still several things missing from this animation, such as a background, motion from the characters, sound track, and the rest of what makes it come alive. Not only that, but your bird probably appears to have popped up out of nowhere a hundred frames or so into the animation. You can make the bird hold a constant position for the duration of the animation by following this procedure:

1. Copy the bird's first frame by clicking the frame and typing Command-C.

2. Paste this frame into frame 1 in the bird's channel by clicking frame 1 and typing Command-V.

3. Select the first and last frames of this sequence and interpolate the intermediate frames, as described in step 9, above.

By structuring your animated scenes in this way, you identify a strong dramatic action—the cat's stalk and pounce. Then you can build other elements around it that heighten the drama—the cat's tail wiggling, the bird bobbing its head up and down, ignorant of the danger. Adding the details becomes much easier after you've got the basic motion in place, just the way fleshing out an outline makes it easier to write a story.

Synchronizing Other Motion

The animation you just created may look a little lifeless. If you rigorously followed the instructions, it's essentially cut-out animation. There's no twitching of the cat's tail, no flapping of the bird's wings, no idle pecking at the ground as the cat prowls, no shuffling of padded paws as the predator wriggles forward in its deadly crouch.

Fortunately, it's easy to build in frame-by-frame animation (as discussed at the end of Chapter 4) once you've blocked out the rough motion with real-time animation. To recap the basics of frame-by-frame animation, it's easiest if you copy the cast member you've already used into a new member in the Cast window. Then you can modify that cast member and keep some visual similarity between the original and the modified version. Figure 6.1 shows how this might look.

In Figure 6.1, cast member 1 is the initial drawing of the cat, positioned in this frame so that she's just beginning to creep on stage. Cast members 5, 6, 7, and 8 show the cat twitching her tail in anticipation of the hunt; likewise, cast members 10, 11, and 12 show the bird innocently pecking at the ground.

To add these animation frames into the motion we've already specified, you need to find a location in the scene where it would look good. For the cat's tail, we want to select a frame where the

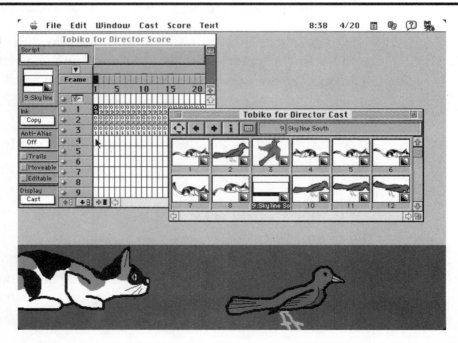

Figure 6.1
Cast members modified from the original

whole cat is visible—it wouldn't do any good to animate the tail in the frame shown in Figure 6.1, for instance.

Traditional animators work out the motion of a sequence by drawing the individual poses in a piece of motion on separate sheets of paper. Then they flip the pages in their hands, rolling them back and forth to see how smoothly the motion progresses from one pose to the next. In Director, you can use the Paint tool to sketch the individual poses, but Director does the flipping back and forth for you as you work on the scene.

Now that you have determined the cat's basic "flight path," you need to add some details that give your movie life. The most important one is familiar to anyone who has ever seen a cat flip its tail: The motion is fairly jerky and rapid in real life. We don't need a fluid motion; the lashing of a cat's tail typically does include wide, radical shifts in position as shown between cast members 6 and 7, for instance.

Timing, Tuning, and Tweaking

Now it's time to start inserting these animated effects into the channel you have assigned to each character. To do that, start looking at the timing of individual frames so you can tune and tweak the action of your movie on a frame by frame basis.

There are two ways you can move from frame to frame to see where you want to insert character motion. One way is simply to click on successive frames in the Score window, so that you can see the amount by which each character moves. The other way is to call up the Control panel, as shown in Figure 6.2, and use the step forward and step backward buttons to move frame by frame.

Clicking once on either of these buttons moves Director's playback head to the adjacent frame, in the direction of the arrow. Alternatively, you can select frames individually from the Score window. Figure 6.3 illustrates a number of components of the Score window as well as other parts of Director that can help you synchronize your motion.

Figure 6.2
The Control panel

Step backward   Step forward

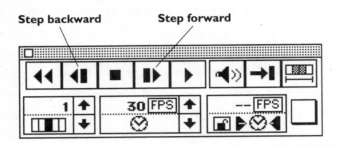

Figure 6.3
Synchronization elements of Director screen

Selected frames   Playback head   Selected cast member

Handles

In Figure 6.3, the Score window shows that the Playback head is on frame 57. Furthermore, the cast member in channel 2 of that frame has been selected; that's cast member 12, the drawing of the

robin in the lowest position of its motion. Frame 54 contains cast
member 2, the still robin; frame 55 contains cast member 10, followed by 11, 12, then 11 and 10 again to give the motion of the
robin's head bobbing down and then back up.

Making and inserting cast members 10 through 12 at the appropriate part of the movie took two separate actions: creating the motion,
then synchronizing it with the rest of the frames. To create the motion,
I first selected just the robin's head with the rectangle, then chose Free
Rotate from the Effects menu. This lets you grab any corner of the rectangle and rotate it into a new position. The robin's beak needed to be
turned a few degrees toward the ground before he could tilt on his feet.
Figure 6.4 shows the robin with his head in the new pose. You will
probably have to fill in some of the details where the head and the
body come together, retouching the edges and refilling the color.

Figure 6.4
The robin
begins his bob

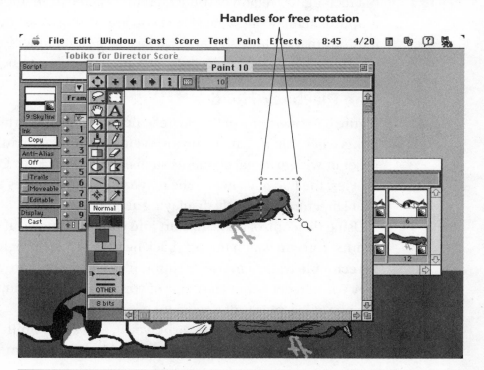

Frames 11 and 12 are successive rotations of the whole robin, performed the same way but with the whole character selected before rotating. You can grab any of the handles to rotate the selected region.

Once you have created the animation, it's time to place those cast members into the robin's channel. When you first drag cast member 10 into a frame that has cast member 2 in it, Director puts the new cast member in the center of the frame. You will then need to drag the new cast member into the same position on the screen as the original.

The trick here is that Director doesn't simply replace what's on the Stage with the new character when you drag in the new cast member. The old cast member (member 2) stays in its position, and in fact its handles still show up if you selected that frame first. These handles are a great cue for lining up your new cast member with the position of the old one, at least for a case such as this. In this case, the rectangular region of the screen that each cast member occupies is approximately the same size. If you are scaling a cast member, or if the animation in each frame causes the cast member to change size, the handles may have little bearing from frame to frame.

The Playback Head

Figure 6.3 shows one of the Score window's most important components when you're synchronizing events on the stage with one another or with external elements such as sound tracks or QuickTime movies: the playback head. The playback head indicates the frame that Director is currently displaying at any time.

Using the control panel to start and stop your movie at different points, you can watch the playback head to see the progress of your Director file while a movie or sound plays in the background. This way you can cue other elements of your movie to appear, move, or change at key points of a segment of external media.

There are some restrictions, however, and some limits to what you can do this way. The main problem is that the frame rate varies depending on a number of elements, most importantly the speed of the processor on which you play back the Director movie. If you move your Director presentation to a machine with a faster or slower processor, you'll see that different elements of the original scene appear, move, and change at different rates. How do you work around this? There are two extremes. One is to limit the kind of processor on which you plan to replay your movie. This is practical only if you are specifying a multimedia kiosk or if you are making a presentation that will be shown only on your company's internal computers or in other cases where you can guarantee control over the processor speed. Also, of course, if you are using Director for an educational project that will run only on one computer in the class-room or the school's computer lab, you can ignore the issue of slower (or, unfortunately, faster) processors. If, however, you are planning to distribute your Director presentation to a wider audi-ence—whether as a no-cost marketing presentation such as an in-teractive brochure, or as an over-the-counter consumer multimedia title—you'll need to make some provision for running your movie at a different speed.

This leads to the other extreme: If you can't guarantee control over the kind of processor used, you have to write for the lowest common denominator. Unlike television scripts, in this case the lowest com-mon denominator is the slowest kind of computer you expect your audience to have. You'll need to make this clear to the intended user on the packaging or media of your Director movie, or of course in the ubiquitous "Read Me First" files on your product's disk or CD-ROM.

This, of course, means testing on Macintosh IIs, on 386 PCs, or whatever you think the bottleneck will be for your audience. You can't speed up the playback on slower machines, but you can slow it down on faster ones to make sure that events happen at the right time. This may mean dropping frames from your original animation if the playback speed gets too slow to support proper timing or to match sound effects. Remember that sound and QuickTime movies always play back at full speed; the gating factor in your Director movies will be scene complexity.

Avoiding unnecessarily complex scenes is another reason that it's good to start designing each scene with the central motion, the piece of animation that drives the dramatic action of the shot. It's much easier to build a simple scene from the beginning, one that takes into account the other elements, than it is to edit a scene later by cutting frames, changing bitmap sizes, and the rest. You can do all those things as necessary to get the timing right and the pace correct, but once again it's the case that a day spent thinking without working saves four days spent working without thinking.

The time, however, will come when you have to adjust, modify, tweak, and tune the playback. And when that time comes, you'll want to learn about the topmost channel of the Score window. This is Director's Tempo channel, and it allows you to slow down scenes to make sure there's enough time for effects, sounds, or other media. You can also use the Tempo channel to pause, wait for mouse clicks, and otherwise control the timing with which your movie plays. The Tempo channel can even add a kind of rudimentary or imitation interactivity to your document, by letting the presentation wait until the user clicks the mouse. (For an introduction to real interactivity, where your user selects elements on the screen and the Director movie goes to different frames or takes different actions, read Chapter 7.)

The Tempo Channel

One of the best aspects of the Tempo channel is that it applies to the individual frames of your movie. If you have one frame that takes a while to build, or one frame within which you have a QuickTime movie or a sound track element playing, you can use the Tempo channel to make your movie wait before continuing with other visual elements. Then on subsequent frames you can return to the preset frame rate of the rest of your title.

In effect, then, the tempo is like applying the brakes to a coasting car: You can slow it down, but you can't speed it up. But how does Director determine the basic frame rate of your movie? Director looks in the frame rate setting of the Control panel, shown in Figure 6.5. This means adding something else to the list of things to check, set, and clarify before beginning to work on your document. (A checklist of these items is included in Appendix B.)

The display toggles let you choose whether to show the frame rate and actual speed as frames per second, or as seconds per frame. Additionally, the Actual Speed display toggle lets you see two other figures:

- Sum, a quick but rough summary of the elapsed time between the beginning of your movie and the current frame

- Est, a slower but more accurate estimate of the elapsed time

Selecting Est can slow playback, because Director has to calculate the elapsed time by counting from the actual frame durations. Be sure to set this toggle back to FPS or to Sum before playing your movie.

Figure 6.6 shows an example of where programmed frame rate and performed frame rate can differ. In the control panel display at

Figure 6.5
The frame rate displays in the control panel

Tempo   Actual frame rate

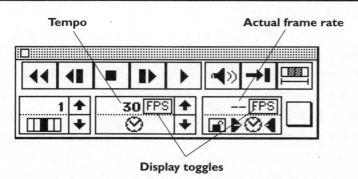

Display toggles

Figure 6.6
A complex frame with several kinds of animation in it

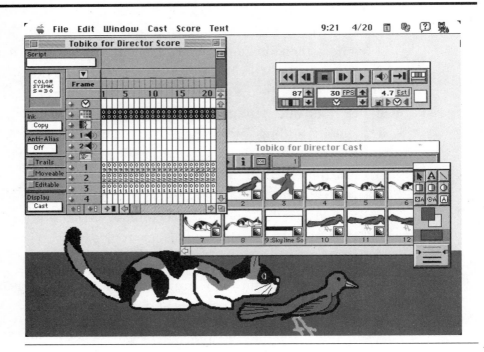

the top right, you can see that the actual frame rate is 4.7 frames per second, even though the tempo is set to 30 fps for this scene. The Score window indicates some of what the difference is: This is the scene in which the cat's tail is being animated, and Director has to swap that Cast member into the scene on successive frames. This slows down the animation from the original tempo of 30 fps to the actual rate of 4.7 fps.

From this example, it's apparent that if you calculate the playback time of a sound effect or QuickTime movie and multiply it by 30 to get the estimated frame count for something to happen at the end of the movie, you can be off by a significant amount if you have complex animations or transformations occurring on the stage. In this example, the cat's tail twitching sequence takes up four frames at an average of just under 5 fps, for about ⅘ of a second total duration. Yet ⅘ of a second at 30 fps is 24 frames. This means that if you try to synchronize a sound or a QuickTime movie to the twitching of the cat's tail, you'll be off by about 19 frames at the end of this sequence. 19 frames is almost ⅔ of a second at the tempo you've selected, but it's almost four seconds at the actual frame rate. Either way, you're going to end up in trouble in short order.

How can setting the Tempo in an individual frame help you with this? You need to determine how slowly the slowest computer you expect to use will display the scenes you're worried about, then you can lock the playback to that speed so that Director will never play those frames back faster, no matter what killer computer you end up using. This way, even if you play the movie on a Power Macintosh or a Pentium-based PC, the frame rate will never exceed the pace you set here.

Here's the procedure for calculating playback rate:

1. Run your movie on a slower computer. Copy the Director file and all its associated elements—sounds, graphics, and the rest— into the computer you're planning to use to test for slow playback. Run the movie through to determine how fast (or how slowly) it plays back, watching the frames per second in the Actual Frame Rate window (as indicated in Figure 6.5).

2. Adjust your frames as required for the new frame rate. You can control playback speed in three ways:

- Reducing the number of sprites you are moving on the stage at any time

- Reducing the bit depth of the sprites on the stage

- Reducing the number of frames your movie displays in a given piece of animation

Depending on the most critical part of your scene, you may wish to choose one of the following options. To evaluate which one is right, consider the most important part of your scene.

■ Is it the action between characters? Then change the number of sprites last; try setting the bit depth of your Cast members to a lower value.

■ Is it the colors of the elements on the screen? Then the bit depth is probably not adjustable. See if there are ways you can consolidate cast members into a single image—for instance, putting several trees or other elements into a single background.

■ Is it smooth motion that simulates a physical process? Then the number of frames may not be negotiable; change the color depth or the number of sprites.

■ Is it synchronization to an external piece of media such as a sound clip? Then see if it's possible to put some of your sound and motion into a QuickTime movie to keep the tightest possible synchronization.

3. Lock the frame rate. This ensures that Director will not play this sequence any faster, no matter how high-powered a processor you run the movie on. To lock the frame rate, click on the padlock icon in the Actual Frame Rate portion of the control panel, as shown in Figure 6.7.

Figure 6.7
Locking the frame rate in a Director movie

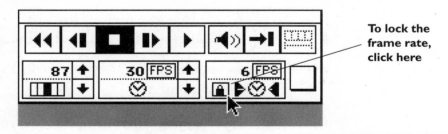

To lock the frame rate, click here

Locking the frame rate of your movie guarantees a known playback rate. It may mean that the playback won't be as fast or as smooth as it will on the fastest computers your customers may be expected to use, but it will mean consistent, synchronized playback no matter what processors your title ends up with.

In addition to letting you set the frame through the control panel, Director gives you a separate Tempo channel in which you can specify the tempo for each frame. The Tempo channel also lets you specify several conditions during which you want Director to wait during the playback of a particular frame or group of frames. Figure 6.8 shows the Set Tempo dialog box.

This dialog box lets you synchronize screen actions, frames of animation, or transitions with sound effects, QuickTime movies, or user input. Sound1 and Sound2 represent, respectively, the sounds in sound channels 1 and 2; you can also make the Director movie wait until the QuickTime file in a specified channel has finished playing. Finally, you can let someone control the pace of the presentation by clicking the mouse or pressing a key to make Director move on to the next scene, frame, or sequence. The following exercise shows how you can use this technique to leave the first frame of a movie visible until the user presses a key.

Figure 6.8
The Set
Tempo
dialog box

> **Set Tempo**
>
> ◉ Tempo: ◁▭▭[30]▭▭▷ fps   [**OK**]
> ○ Wait: ◁[1]▭▭▭▭▷ seconds   [Cancel]
> ○ Wait for Mouse Click or Key
> ○ Wait for Sound1 To Finish
> ○ Wait for Sound2 To Finish
> ○ Wait for Digital Video Movie
>   to Finish in Channel: [1]   [Help]

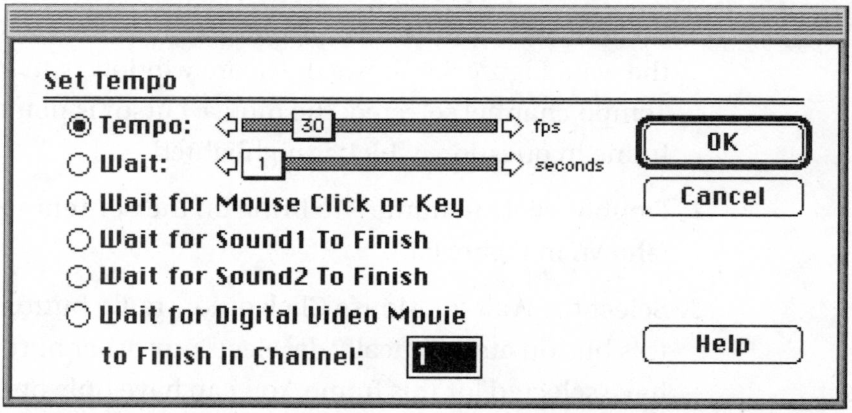

Pausing for a Mouse Click

True interactivity involves letting the user select one of several different options on the screen and following a chosen path. While the next chapter discusses a number of ways of accomplishing interactivity of this kind, the following exercise shows you how to make Director pause until the user presses a key or clicks the mouse. This is a useful technique for timing narration during title development, for example, or for using Director as a presentation aid where there is a live moderator.

This exercise displays the first frame of the Director movie and then waits for user input. You can replicate the exercise anywhere in your document by substituting the frame at which you want the movie to pause. The key is to note that Director will not display the current frame until you press a key—that is, it does not display the frame and wait, it displays the frame only after someone presses the key. That explains the choice of frame in step 1, below:

1. Select frame 2 of the Tempo channel in the Score window. You must select frame 2 because Director interprets the command to begin playing as the keystroke to start frame 1. So to have Director display a frame but hold it till you press a key or click the mouse, you must first display frame 1, then select frame 2 for the wait. Figure 6.9 shows the Score window with frame 2 of the Tempo channel selected; the mouse cursor is pointing to the frame in question, which is highlighted.

2. Double-click on frame 2 to bring up the Set Tempo dialog box (shown in Figure 6.8).

3. Select the Wait for Mouse Click or Key radio button. Selecting this button automatically deselects any other button you may have selected for this frame. You can have only one Tempo button selected per frame.

Figure 6.9
Where to select frame 2 of the Score window

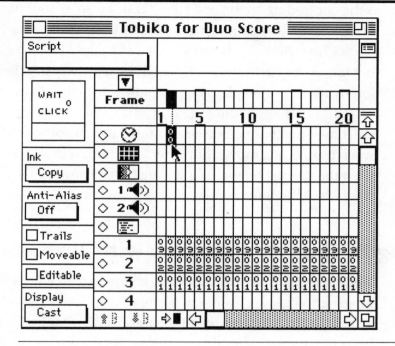

4. Click the OK button. Director adds a double zero to the frame in the Tempo channel.

Now, when you watch your movie, Director will pause after displaying frame 1, waiting until you click the mouse or press a key before continuing.

Note that if you intend to use interactivity in a scene, you should not also set the Wait for Mouse Click or Key button as described in this procedure. If you have multiple selections as described in the following chapter, you need to let them control what and where in your document the user chooses to display.

Additionally, you can use the Set Tempo dialog box to force Director to wait until a sound or a QuickTime movie finishes playing. This gives you one additional way of synchronizing your movie with its internal components. If you want a sound to finish playing before an animation starts, you can choose either of the two sound channels as the controlling factor, and Director will display the current frame till the sound finishes playing. Likewise, if you build a frame to show a QuickTime movie, you can use the Set Tempo dialog box to hold that frame (for example, to display titles, graphics, or other information) while the video plays in a window within that frame.

In addition to providing the Tempo channel, Director lets you use the Transition channel (discussed next) to control the change between frames of a movie. But where the Tempo channel controls when the change happens, the Transition channel controls how it looks when the frames change.

Creating Pseudo-Animations with Transitions

Director lets you use transitions to create special effects when your presentation moves from one frame to another. Without transitions, all changes from one frame to the next in Director happen simply by replacing the old with the new. While this is what you want for animation, where the whole point is to make an invisible change from each pose of a character to the next, there are times when you might wish to signify a change in mood, direction, dramatic content, or location in the information set.

Transitions typically move, change, or display different portions of the successive frames in some kind of a pattern. For example, you can push the old frame off the bottom of the screen while the new frame slides in from the top. Alternatively, you can make the new frame appear in a checkerboard pattern underneath the old frame. Or you can fade from one frame to the next. Director has 52 different transitions in version 4.0.4.

Director uses a specific channel to store transitions from frame to frame. Figure 6.10 shows the Transition channel. To select a transition, double-click on the cell of the frame to which you want to add the transition.

Figure 6.10
Director's
Transition
channel in the
Score window

**Transition
channel**

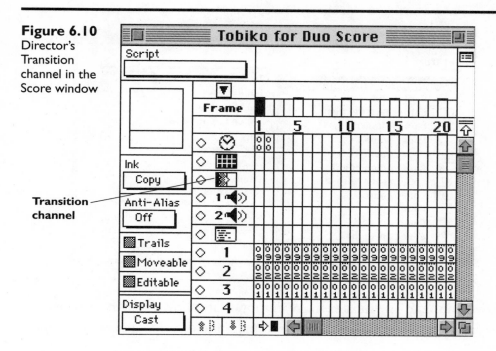

Note that transitions apply at the beginning of a frame, not at the end. That is, if you select a transition for frame 10, Director displays frame 9 first, then displays the transition, then displays frame 10. This way you can use the Tempo channel in frame 9 to make Director wait for a mouse click, then display a transition as a way of introducing frame 10.

When you click on the Transition channel of your Director movie, Director displays the dialog box shown in Figure 6.11.

In addition to managing the transition between scenes, you can use some transitions to provide visual effects as you introduce new cast members. The trick is that some transitions affect the whole screen image, pushing the old image aside as the new image comes into view. Other transitions, however, replace the old image with pieces of the new frame already in place. And because of the way animation works with persistence of vision, the effect is as if you were only making the new portions of the frame appear, or old ones

Figure 6.11
The Director
Transition
dialog box

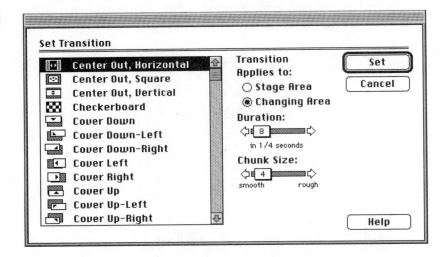

disappear. The next exercise demonstrates how you can use this technique to make characters appear and disappear within a scene.

"Beaming In" and "Beaming Out" Your Characters

For this exercise, you'll need a couple of different graphical elements—a character and a background image—to see how transitions can make things seem to appear and disappear. The snapshot uses our cheerleading Tooth Fairy as the character, and an abstract pattern of rectangles as the background.

1. Make the background image persist on the stage. To do this, drag the background image from the Cast into the Score, in channel 1. Place it in at least three cells in channel 1 so that you can see your character appear and disappear.

2. Place the character in frame 2 of channel 2. Remember to set the Ink style to Matte so that the slug behind your character doesn't cover the background image. This makes frame 2 look something like the figure on the next page.

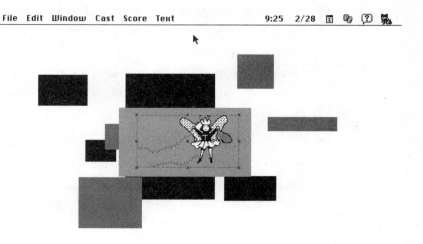

A Few Observations about Transitions and Synchronization

Don't put a tempo switch and a transition in the same frame. Director transitions happen independently of frame motion and frame-by-frame animation, and I believe Director's documentation simply gives the usual vague warning about "unexpected results" if you combine the two. That warning has always been good enough for me; the results I expect are often scary enough that I'm happy to be cautious about unexpected ones.

Because transitions happen outside of the normal calculation of time by frame count, you need to be careful to start sounds, QuickTime movies, and other real-time effects after a transition finishes. Finish a transition first, then start a new sound effect. And be aware that if you have a transition in the middle of a looping sound such as music in the background channel of a slide presentation, expect variable duration. You can't be sure how long the transition will take when you move the Director file to another computer, so don't expect to have tightly cued motion and audio if there's a transition in the middle of the scene.

Remember that waiting for a mouse click occurs at the end of a frame, while transitions occur at the beginning. In the fairy example, for instance, you can add a Wait for Mouse Click to your Tempo channel in frame 2, in which case the fairy sparkles onto the scene and remains visible till you click the mouse (or press a key). Then she disappears.

3. Select the Transition channel for frame 2. To do this, expose the Score window, scrolling up to the transition channel if necessary. (The Transition channel is the third channel from the top, two below the Tempo channel discussed previously in this chapter.) When you double-click on the Transition channel for this frame, Director displays the Set Transition dialog box.

4. Choose Dissolve, Pixels from the Set Transition dialog box. Additionally, set the Duration slider to 8. To determine the duration, multiply the number you select times increments of ¼ second; a duration of 8 makes the fairy sparkle into the scene over a period of two seconds.

5. Watch your movie! Command-1 clears the stage, Command-R rewinds the movie, and Command-P plays it. You should see the background image in frame 1, with the fairy sparkling over the rectangles for two seconds in frame 2. Then, of course, the fairy disappears entirely in frame 3.

6. Make the Tooth Fairy beam out of the scene. By now you should know how to do this: Select the Transition channel for frame 3, choose Dissolve, Pixels with a duration of 8, and then watch your movie. Now the Tooth Fairy should sparkle onto the scene in frame 2, then disappear with sparkles in frame 3. At the end of the last frame you should see only the rectangles.

Endnote on Synchronizing Sound and Motion

To recap, processing speeds vary from computer to computer. In broadcast video and motion pictures, the relationship between media developer and media consumer is strictly that of master and slave—at least insofar as timing and synchronization is concerned. Broadcasters distribute media at fixed frame rates, rates that are specified by the producer of the content. The players for motion pictures all synchronize at 24 frames per second and do not vary from that; the players for broadcast video all synchronize at 30 frames per second, using 60 fields of odd and even lines down the television image. Computer multimedia has to contend with different computers, different configurations, and different user expectations.

The surest way to synchronize sound, motion, and pictures is to use a digital video format such as QuickTime, QuickTime for Windows, or Microsoft Video for Windows. These standards are the closest to providing the kind of synchronization that the movie and television industries have been developing since the late 1920s. This comparison to technology of the early part of this century should give you an idea about why computer multimedia synchronization in the mid-1990s lags behind the entertainment industry. QuickTime was first introduced in 1992; the timing mechanisms used by Hollywood have been in development since the production of *The Jazz Singer* in 1927. Furthermore, motion pictures and television have the benefit of standardized playback devices, devices that do not introduce the variable of processing speed into the picture.

Is this an industry apology for poor performance? I hope not. Does it get you thinking about how to work around the current state of the market, as well as the art? I hope so. Do I also hope it makes you begin to imagine what might be possible in the future, as the digital video industry develops synchronization standards comparable to and compatible with the Society of Motion Pictures and Television Engineers (SMPTE) code, the standard for broadcast video? Yes indeed.

For now, the best way to work around the variables in playback speed and synchronization is to work in small, discrete modules of information. Keep sound clips short, use video when possible, and synchronize your scenes in a new way: by event rather than by time. Fortunately, computer multimedia provides a means of synchronizing by event and by module that broadcast media can't begin to match. Better still, this means of synchronization provides users with a power, flexibility, and degree of control that's unimaginable in traditional media. This means of synchronization is, of course, interactivity.

The next chapter is dedicated to understanding interactivity: how to plan for it, how to provide it, and most important, how to control it with Director's scripting language, Lingo.

CHAPTER

7

Lingo: Strategies for Interactivity

Director uses a group of instructions called a *script* to control the flow of your document. *Lingo* is the name of the language in which scripts are written.

Some of the initial users of interactivity tools such as HyperCard were intimidated by the prospect of writing programs. For this reason, in the early days of interactivity, the word "script" was adopted to avoid frightening people by using the word "program." So instead of programs, they were only expected to write scripts that instructed the computer in what card to display, what action to take, what transition to make from card to card, and the like. Of course, now everyone sees through the ruse, and most people are just as afraid of writing scripts as they were of writing programs.

Script writing, like programming, is viewed as a specialized skill full of hard-to-remember jargon, accessible only after years and years of study and dedication. Its jargon can be hard to remember, but only if you don't use the vocabulary all the time. The trick to approaching scripts is to understand that when it comes to interactivity, there are only seven scripting statements you really need to know in order to add interactivity to a title. Familiarity and practice with these seven scripting statements will have you designing interactive documents in a very short period of time.

What Is a Script?

A script is a sequence of instructions that tells Director to do something. These instructions are written in a kind of English shorthand that includes commands to do things such as:

- Start playing the movie at a specified frame
- Keep displaying the current frame until another instruction is received

■ Check to see whether a certain event, such as a mouse click, has happened

In its entirety, Lingo is a powerful and flexible method of controlling many elements of your Director movie. All Lingo scripts contain these English-like commands, but some scripts can be very elegant, complicated, and difficult to design.

The Seven Basic Lingo Commands

For the purpose of this chapter, we'll study only the seven Lingo commands you need to know:

■ MouseUp

■ MouseDown

■ ExitFrame

■ EnterFrame

■ Go to frame #

■ Play frame #

■ End

Writing in such code words, you can give Director instructions that tell it what to do when certain events happen in certain conditions in your document. For example, in Chapter 6 you used the Tempo channel to make Director pause until the user pressed a key or clicked the mouse. You can also write a Director script to pause when it has finished playing a certain frame in your movie. The following script has that effect:

```
on exitFrame
    pause
end
```

This script tells Director, "When you finish playing the current frame, pause until further notice with that frame still displayed." The word end on the last line tells Director that the script is over; otherwise, Director would continue looking through your computer's memory and try to perform whatever it found in the next slot in RAM. You will use a script just like this one often when you design interactive presentations with Director. You will probably include such a script in every frame that contains a menu or a set of navigation buttons. In fact, it's a good idea to write this once in your cast and then copy it into each of the frames in which you require it.

The Script's Theater of Operation

The script I used as the preceding example affects the entire Director movie. However, its *scope* is the frame in which you assign it. Borrowing from Director's drama-oriented naming conventions, I say that this script's "theater of operation" is the frame. It's important that you distinguish the different theaters of operation in Director: the frame, the sprite, and the cast member.

You can attach a script to a frame, a cast member, or a sprite. That script will then have its own unique scope, or theater of operation, that changes how the script affects your movie. The theater of operation affects the time and space within which the script is active.

As a practical matter, use frame scripts to pause the entire flow of the movie. Use cast member scripts for standard buttons, effects, or other actions that you want to be identical no matter where or when they appear in your movie. Use sprite scripts when you want something that looks the same (that is, uses the same cast member) but changes its effect from time to time.

Attaching a Script to a Frame

Scripts attached to a frame occur within that frame of the Director movie. The previous example (making the movie pause when

Director exits the current frame) is a frame script; its scope is the whole frame. It requires no further interactivity than that; when Director displays that frame, it reads this script. Later, when Director exits that frame, it executes the script and pauses the display as it stands at the end of that frame.

To attach a script to a frame, click on the cell in the Script channel that indicates the frame in which you want the script to be active. Then pull down the Script panel and select New, as illustrated in Figure 7.1. The Director Script window, shown in Figure 7.2, pops up.

Figure 7.1
Attaching a script to a frame in the Score window

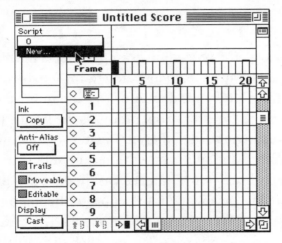

Figure 7.2
The Script editor

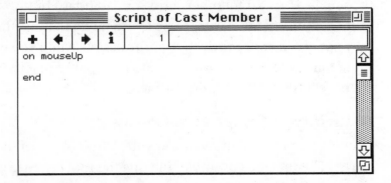

Director adds the first and last lines of the script when it opens the editor for you. In this script, Director begins with the assumption that you want your script to take effect after a mouse click. This is the default, or automatic, assumption for scripts whose theater of operation is the frame. You may instead wish to write a script that takes effect when Director first enters this frame, or when Director has finished drawing everything in the frame and the playback head exits it. You can change the first line (which describes the condition required for execution) by deleting the word MouseUp and replacing it with one of the other three conditions you might use for designing an interactive document (which I'll describe in the next few sections of this chapter).

Attaching Scripts to Sprites and Cast Members

Attaching scripts to sprites and cast members differs in small but significant ways. Remember that when you drag a cast member into the score, Director places a sprite for that cast member on the stage, but only in the frame into which you dragged the cast member. The sprite contains information specific to that frame, such as its location on the stage; this information may vary from frame to frame. For instance, when you animate a sprite to move across the stage, its position information is different from frame to frame, while the cast member does not change.

A script attached to a sprite, then, only has that individual frame as its theater of operation. For example, you can define a button that is only active for a limited period of time, by attaching the script to the sprite. The script only works in the frames in which you attached the script to that sprite. This way, it's possible to have a limited amount of time within which your users can make a selection before the script "times out." You can use this technique to display automatic help screens; if the user doesn't make a selection within some time value you choose (say, 30 seconds), you can display instructions or play a sound clip that helps them decide what to do.

A script attached to a cast member, on the other hand, is available any time you display that cast member. Cast-member scripts are a good way to define standard buttons that always do the same thing. For example, if you have a basic navigation button that takes you to the overview screen or table of contents for your Director title, or a Help button that always jumps to the same page, you can attach the cast member to a Lingo script that jumps to the frame where the help screens begin. However, both sprite scripts and cast member scripts apply only within the physical boundaries of the object that you draw, unlike the frame script, which applies within the physical boundaries of the frame itself. To understand what this means, consider the following imaginary script:

```
on mouseUp
    [do something...]
end
```

The same script does the following different things for each of the three theaters of operation in which you might define a script:

- Frame script: as soon as the mouse comes up, no matter where the mouse is located, but only in this frame.

- Cast member script: as soon as the mouse comes up, only within the boundaries of the drawing that represents this cast member, and in any frame in which this cast member appears.

- Sprite script: as soon as the mouse comes up, only within the boundaries of the drawing that represents this sprite, and only in the specific frame in which this sprite appears.

The best way to understand the difference between a sprite script and a cast member script is to consider the difference between a button that takes you to the table of contents, and a button that takes you to the next page. The Table of Contents button would be a cast member script, because the table of contents is always in the same place in your movie. The Next Page button, on the other hand, takes you to a different place in your movie each time you put it on the stage, but it needs to have the same appearance for usability's sake. If you implement your Next Page button as a sprite script, you can use the same cast member every time you drag it into the score, but you can give it a unique script that jumps to wherever the next page is located in your document.

The Three Command Categories

Lingo as a full-fledged programming language contains more than a hundred commands. Earlier in this chapter, you were introduced to the seven commands that are essential for adding interactivity to your movies. To make it even easier, there are three categories into which these commands fall:

- Conditions—what has to happen for Director to execute this script, given the theater of operation in which this script takes effect

- Branching—the command telling Director what part of the movie to execute next

- Closing—telling Director that the script in question is over

You construct scripts in the order that the categories are presented here: You begin with a condition, you specify the branching operation, and then you close the script. The example you have already seen is a simple, but often-used, Director script that demonstrates this pattern.

The following sections explain each of the seven pertinent Lingo commands within the context of the categories described below.

Conditions: Checking the Mouse and the Frame

You can define the conditions under which the Lingo script will be executed with one of the following four commands:

■ On MouseUp—wait until the user lets up on the mouse button, then perform the rest of the script. On MouseUp is the command you use to execute a mouse-click; it signifies that the user has pushed down on the mouse, then let up on it.

■ On MouseDown—wait until the user presses down on the mouse button, then perform the rest of the script. On MouseDown is the command you use to initiate a drag, or to change color indicating that the user has selected something.

■ On EnterFrame—run the following script as soon as the playback head enters the frame. On EnterFrame is the command you use to perform any background programming information required before displaying objects on the screen; we won't use it for any of the examples here, but it provides balance for the following command.

■ On ExitFrame—wait until Director has displayed the entire frame, including all animation and sound effects; then, as the playback head leaves this frame (but before it enters the following frame), perform the commands in the rest of this script. On ExitFrame is the command you use to pause a Director movie while waiting for the user to select one of several choices from a menu, a table of contents, or some other navigation scheme.

As a very, very general rule, you'll find that most of your scripts for which the theater of operation is the frame will begin with on ExitFrame or on EnterFrame. Likewise, on MouseUp will probably be the opening line of scripts associated with either sprites or cast members. On MouseDown is the appropriate opening for sprite scripts, where you may wish to do something the instant the user presses down on the mouse such as change the color of the sprite to indicate that it has been selected.

Branching: Where Will I Go? What Will I Do?

Once the condition defined in the first line has been met, Director executes the subsequent lines of the script one at a time. You can define interactivity with nothing more than a condition (On MouseUp) and a branching statement (do something), followed by the closing statement.

What you do depends on how you have structured your Director movie's interactivity. The two options discussed here give you a choice of two different schemes of managing flow:

```
go to frame #
play frame #
```

The difference between Go to frame # and Play frame # is subtle, but significant. Telling a script to go to frame 120 sends the playback head to frame 120, and movie play continues from that point until it encounters a pause or the end of the movie. To bring the playback head to another part of the movie, you must pause the movie with on ExitFrame pause (as described in the previous example), while you display the options that your user can take at this point. Go to frame # is effectively a one-way jump.

Play frame #, on the other hand, causes the playback head to play a defined sequence of frames, then return to the point where the Play frame command was issued. There are two additional pieces of information you need to know: where Director returns, and how it knows that the defined sequence of frames is done.

If the Play frame # command is issued from a frame script, the playback head returns to the frame that follows the one containing the Play frame # command. For example, if frame 5 contains a script with the command Play frame 120, Director plays the sequence of frames beginning at 120 and then returns to frame 6. If the Play frame # command is issued from a sprite script, Director returns to the frame containing the script. For example, if frame 10 contains a script with the command Play frame 140, Director displays the sequence of frames beginning at frame 140, then returns to frame 10.

But how does it know when the sequence beginning at frame 140 is done? There's one additional command you'll need to learn if you use the Play frame # statement, but it's really simple: Play done. To signify the end of a sequence of frames, add the following script to the last frame of that sequence:

```
on exitFrame
    play done
end
```

You can use the Play frame #/Play done structure to give help instructions, to add information, or to perform any kind of branching where you only want your audience to return to the frame from which they began.

Closing: That's All, Folks

The closing statement is the simplest part of programming. There's only one option, and it's eminently obvious: the command is End.

Here then are some typical scripts, with an explanation of what they do and when you might use them.

```
on exitFrame
    play frame 251
end
```

The preceding script, which probably uses the frame as its theater of operation, waits till the current frame is finished, then does a jump-and-return to frame 251. Sometime after frame 251 plays, your document will display a frame that contains the following script:

```
on exitFrame
    play done
end
```

The preceding script returns the playback head to the appropriate point in the movie—either to the frame after the one from which it was called (if it was called from a frame script) or the frame from which it was called (if it was called from a sprite script).

```
on mouseUp
    go to frame 400
end
```

The preceding script, which probably uses either a sprite or a cast member as its theater of operation, puts the playback head at frame 400 when the user lets up on the mouse (completing a click).

Frame Numbers versus Frame Markers

In the examples shown so far, I've used the # sign to indicate the frame to which you send the playback head in the branching statements. In practice, this can be a questionable strategy for interactivity. There are three problems with it, all boiling down to confusion.

Why Using Frame Numbers Is a Bad Idea

First, using a frame number introduces the risk of confusion if you delete, move, or add frames before the frame number to which you send the playback head. Let's say you set up a jump to frame 150. Then you decide to add a section of movie after frame 100, including a cute new effect that someone came up with. You add thirty frames. Now frame 150 is actually frame 180, but your jump to frame 150 still points to the old number. Director will dutifully begin playing at frame 150, and the movie will probably not look the way you expected it to look.

Second, using a frame number risks confusion when you are trying to follow the logical flow of your document based on the Lingo scripts. If you have a script that's full of jumps to numbered frames, you'll have no way of knowing by reading the Lingo script what is supposed to be displaying when the user clicks on the object associated with the script.

Third, Director has no way of telling you what frame numbers you have chosen as the destination for your jumps. If you write your Lingo scripts in such a manner that they jump to numbered frames in your document, the scripts provide no way of letting you check through them to see what numbers you have specified. This can cause you problems in development: If you are trying to figure out why an interactive movie doesn't do what you expected, you have no way of looking over the list of frames to which you send a user. You'll have to look at all the scripts one by one.

Using Frame Markers—A Better Approach

Fortunately, Director provides a way around all these problems: by naming individual frames with markers. You can use the name that you associate with the marker to direct flow to an individual frame. You can give the marker an understandable, English name, including spaces and with a practically limitless number of characters. I've tested it with up to 130 characters, to see whether there was an upper limit, and got tired of typing before I heard it beep at me to tell me I'd reached the limit. However, keeping names to a dozen or so characters is probably a good idea for a number of reasons. First, that's about all that Director will display in the Markers window (12 characters plus an ellipsis), and second, you don't want to have to type more than that many characters (much less remember them) when you refer to a marker.

How does it work? To place a marker in your movie, drag a marker from the marker well and position it over the frame of the movie that you wish to mark. Figure 7.3 shows this.

Figure 7.3
The Marker well and a marked frame

The Marker well

A frame marker in place

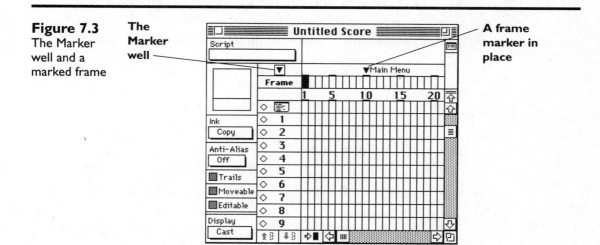

After you drag the marker to its position over the frame you wish to mark, Director gives you a flashing cursor to the right of the marker. At that point, you can type in any marker name you wish. You can use spaces, you can go up to 130 characters and possibly more, but for all the reasons previously mentioned it's best to keep your marker names short and easy to read.

How Marker Names Work

There are two ways you can use marker names to make working in Director easier:

■ Use them in your Lingo scripts as the destination for one of the branching statements, Go to frame "Marker Name" or Play "Marker Name"

■ Select them from the Marker window and jump directly to the frame in your document that you have marked

Here's how each of these techniques works.

In your Lingo scripts, you can use the marker name instead of the frame number. For example, to jump to frame 10 in Figure 7.3 when the user clicks an object, add the following script to that object's cast member:

```
on mouseUp
    go to frame "Main Menu"
end
```

This script should probably have the cast member as its theater of operation, rather than a sprite or a frame, because you probably want to use the same button everywhere in your movie to send people to the main menu.

If you notice something goofy on a particular frame while you're playing back your movie, you can pull down the Window menu and select Markers, as shown in Figure 7.4.

Figure 7.4
Selecting the Markers option from the Window menu

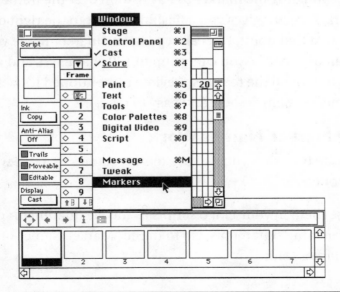

When you select Markers, Director displays the Markers window. This lists all the markers you have placed in your document. The list in the Markers window is mouse-sensitive; to select the frame in your movie that corresponds to one of the markers, click on that marker in the left-hand side of the list. Figure 7.5 illustrates this.

Figure 7.5
Choosing a frame from the Markers window

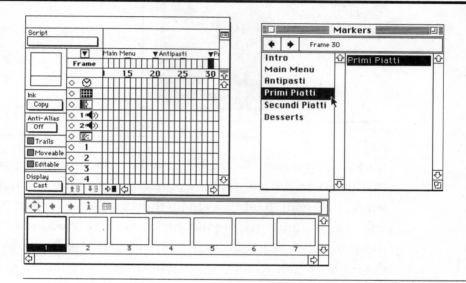

Figure 7.5 illustrates having selected the frame marked "Primi Piatti" from the list of available markers. Note that in the Score window, the playback head is in frame 30, and that the words "Frame 30" appear above the list of markers.

You can also write comments in the right-hand field of the Markers window. When you first give a marker a name, that name shows up in the comments window. To add a comment, put the cursor after the name of the marker, press the Return key, and then type the comment. Figure 7.6 shows this for another marker.

In short, markers provide you with a way of communicating information inside your Director movie. You may for example use the comments in markers to convey information about the content of

Figure 7.6
Comments in
a Markers
window

the frame. You may also wish to use the comments to convey information about the status of the project, or other information that
would be useful to other team members working on that movie with
you. And the ability to use the marker column as a kind of hypertext
index to the marked frames of your movie makes it easy for you to
determine where to send the playback head in your Lingo scripts.

Later in the chapter we'll do some exercises to help you see how
good planning of interactivity makes it easier to add interactivity to
your movie at a later date. For now, let's examine how to use some
typical Lingo scripts for turning visual elements of your movie into
buttons that control interactivity.

Creating Buttons from Scripts

You're probably already familiar with interactive programs full of
buttons, text-laden areas done in three dimensions to look like they
were chiseled from marble or made from brushed stainless steel.
With a simple Lingo script, you can make any cast member into a

button. This means that in addition to making text elements and icons into buttons, you can make photographs, drawings, characters, even animation loops into buttons. Remember the butterfly wings in Chapter 4? They can be a button, available for your user to click on as they flutter across the stage. In Director, if you can see it, you can make a button out of it. Here's how.

1. Select the cast member you want to make into a button. To select a cast member, click once on the member's thumbnail in the Cast window. Figure 7.7 shows the Cast window with member 1 selected.

Figure 7.7
Components of the Cast window

2. With the desired cast member selected, click the Script button, the rightmost button on the tool bar at the top of the Cast window. This opens the Lingo editor for the selected cast member. Figure 7.8 shows the Lingo editor.

The Lingo editor automatically opens with two lines similar to these. Not all Lingo scripts begin with on MouseUp; that condition really only applies when the theater of operation is a cast member or a sprite. When you create a frame script, Director automatically begins it with on ExitFrame.

Figure 7.8
The Lingo
editor when it
first opens

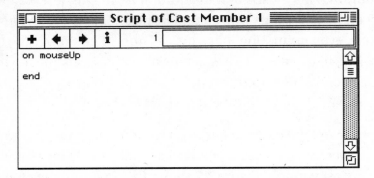

3. Add the desired branching command to the middle line of the
   script.

At this point, you need to consider two questions:

■ What frame comes next? This is where the Marker window can
help you; sensible, understandable names for your markers
make it easy to find the frame to which you want the movie to
jump. Because you can click on the marker's name and display
the stage as it appears at that time, Director makes it easy to see
what else is visible in any of the marked frames.

■ Do you want a Go to or a Play statement for the reference to that
frame? Once again, you can use the Marker window's comments
pane to keep track of whether the frame with the marker has an
associated play done script later in the flow.

There's a little more planning if you're going to use the Play frame
Lingo statement. It can be well worth it, so let's examine some of the
cases in which it's useful.

Planning to Use Play Frame

You may already be familiar with the term modular design. In modular design, the units with which you deal—scenes in a movie, in this case—are comparatively self-contained. The module has a clearly defined beginning, a function that it performs after the beginning, and a clearly defined end. The Play frame sequence lets you define and handle modules in your Director movie. When your movie reaches a Lingo script with a Play frame statement, it jumps to the remote module. This module needs to have a defined beginning, indicated by the marker, and a defined end, indicated by the Play done statement after the last frame in the module. The frames in between can do anything that any other Director sequence can do. Play frame is a good choice when you want to return your audience to the same point in the movie after the remote sequence finishes.

Some people use Play frame to guide their audience to help screens or to short tutorial movies or video clips. Consider also using it when you have a graphical image that you want to remain unchanged while a QuickTime or .AVI file pops up over the screen; when the Director sequence reaches the Play done script, your movie returns to the graphical image. This is a nice way to present short informative movies about places in a city, while the map of the city remains visible and unchanging beneath the video clips. Alternatively, you can make an animated children's book in which the characters on the page are sensitive to the mouse. You can define individual modules that contain the responses you want your audience to see when they click on the individual character.

The real difference between the two ways of jumping to another part of your movie is that Play frame makes it possible to have self-contained modules that can be called from anywhere in the movie—and which will return to the place they were called from. Go to frame is a one-way branch; while you could put another Go to frame later in that movie to define a kind of module, it would always go to the same frame number, no matter where in the movie you invoked this sequence with the Go to frame statement. Figure 7.9 illustrates this.

Figure 7.9
Movie flow in two different schemes

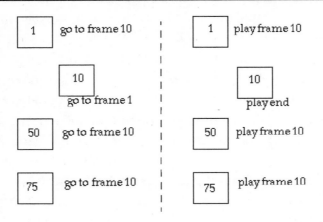

In both of these movies, frame 1 contains a button that causes the movie to play the sequence beginning at frame 10. In both cases, after the sequence of frames beginning at 10 are finished, the movie returns to frame 1. In this case, the two structures are identical.

But when frame 50 contains the button that jumps to frame 10, things get different. In both cases, play begins at frame 10 and continues till the defined end of that sequence. But in the movie on the left, when the frame 10 sequence is done, the movie returns to frame 1 because that value has been written into the script. In the movie on the right, the movie returns to frame 50—the frame that called it—when the sequence starting with frame 10 is done.

The same thing happens for a button clicked in frame 75: When the sequence at frame 10 ends, the one written with Go to frame jumps back to frame 1, while the one written with Play frame returns to frame 75.

Making Menus: Giving Your Buttons Visual Structure

There are several ways to make menus; in the spirit of interface-free design, I'll discuss my favorite way first. My favorite kind of menu doesn't look like a menu: It looks like the things I'm learning about, the game I'm playing, or the story I'm reading. At this end of designing for interactivity, to paraphrase Shakespeare, "All the world's a menu, and all the objects in it merely buttons; they have their hyperlinks and their references, and their little lives are rounded with a click." An interface-free menu for a title about cooking, for example, could start with a photograph, a drawing, or a 3D model of a kitchen, with all the implements, tools, gadgets, and appliances acting as buttons.

In this sense, your title's layout and art direction is itself the visual structure that gives a sense of direction, purpose, and power to your title. The examples in this chapter have shown you how to make cast members into buttons by adding a simple, three-line script to them:

```
on mouseUp
    go to frame "Marker Name"
end
```

Because each button can jump to another frame in your movie, you can nest menus as deeply as you want (being mindful of your audience's ability to find their way around in the twisty little maze of mouse clicks, all alike). The frame you jump to might be identical to the one on display when your user clicked the button, except for whatever activity that button caused to be. For instance, in an interactive storybook for kids, you might choose to set up your scenes so that when the players click on a character, that character performs a little animation while the rest of the frame looks on; then, at the end of the character's dance, you return to the initial frame.

If you're teaching, or if the subject you're presenting is more complex than a storybook, you may want to structure your menus into a kind of hierarchy. You've learned enough to make pop-up menus, where another level of choices appears when your audience clicks on an object in the scene. For example, the kitchen might have a bookshelf in the corner; clicking on the bookshelf could pop up a list of titles, or a list of recipes, which your audience could then select from. Or the food processor could pop up a menu that let your audience choose to see a list of attachments, a short video about how it worked, or a list of recipes that use it.

No matter how many levels of menu or what degree of interactivity you choose for your title, Director handles it in predominantly the same way, with the same basic choices in the Lingo scripts you write. You have to decide the theater of operation for the script; for buttons, you will probably write scripts attached to the cast member. You have to decide where to start playing the movie when your audience clicks on your button. And you have to decide how it appears on the screen, and what cast members are visible.

Simplifying Duplicated Scenes in Remote Locations

Two additional tips can simplify duplicating scenes in remote locations. You can Shift-Click or drag the mouse to select multiple cast members in a frame. For example, Figure 7.10 shows the result of dragging to select the cast members in channels 5, 6, 7, and 8. When all the cells are selected, typing Command-C (or Control-C in Windows) will copy them onto the Clipboard. You can then paste them into any other frame in your document.

If you have 10 or 12 cast members in a given scene, you can drag the mouse to select all of them, copy them to the Clipboard, and then paste them into the new location in one smooth operation. You can then perform whatever your title calls for in that new location. For instance, you can replace one cast member with an animated film loop that shows the character dancing, singing, playing tricks on someone else in the scene, and so on. Additionally, if you tied the scripts to the cast members themselves, they will all be active in the

Figure 7.10
Selecting
multiple cells
to duplicate a
frame's
contents

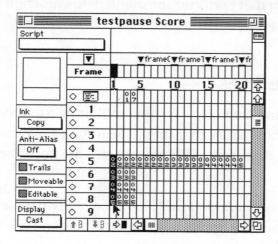

new location just as they were in the original. You can use an on
ExitFrame pause script after your "star" finishes the animation you
selected for him or her, and all the cast members will still be active
buttons. It's pretty slick.

The other tip involves using screen snapshots to copy the appearance of a screen without retaining the individual cast members. You
don't always need all the elements of a scene, particularly if you
want to disable the background when a submenu pops up. One way
to do this is to take a screen snapshot of your Director movie, import
it as a single cast member, and then include it in channel 1 of the new
location. You can even change the appearance of the scene slightly,
for example graying it out in a program like Adobe Illustrator or
Photoshop, or matting over it a 50 percent pattern of gray dots to
lower the intensity of the background scene. Then it's easy to have a
submenu pop up over the background simply by adding the new
cast member for the submenu to channel 2 (or 3, if you put the gray
"mesh" in channel 2). As a result, each menu selection on the popup
will be its own cast member, each in its own channel and with its

own Lingo script that performs the menu item's function when your audience clicks on it.

Establishing Guidelines

Interactivity using Lingo (or any other multimedia authoring tool) boils down to three issues that should be resolved in order to guide your user through your title. These concerns are posed below as questions:

- *Where does each button lead?* This issue has two dimensions. Chapter 1 touched on the first, which is how you use layout and other visual cues (not to mention good clear text) to let your audience know what their control options are at any given time in the title. The second dimension, of course, is the Lingo script; you'll need to consider where you connect the script, to the sprite or to the cast member, and how to send your audience to that part of the movie.

- *Where is the additional information?* While you can send your audience to individual frames by number, that's risky. A better way is to use markers to indicate which frames are the starting points of self-contained sequences. Additionally, you can pull up the Marker window and jump to the specific frames identified by markers in the scrolling pane at the left side of the window. This can be a tremendous aid just during the development of your movie, and for that reason alone would be worth using markers instead of frame numbers.

- *How does Director know that the remote sequence is done, and what happens?* You have three basic ways of responding: You can use the Play frame #/Play done structure to define self-contained modules; you can send your audience unconditionally back to some other frame in the movie when the remote sequence finishes; or you can use on ExitFrame pause to stop your movie's playback and show the audience a menu of choices at that point in the story.

Your document will work better and be more successful if you think about the answers to those questions early on, in the design stage rather than the execution. It's possible to go back and install Play end statements in a linear movie or to break a fluid story into discrete chunks (in fact, that's what chapters in a book and scenes in a play do). But if you're really looking to make your title interactive, you'll need to consider much more than just what we've covered here.

For real interactivity, you need to work from the top down as well as from the bottom up, and you need to start this work at the very beginning of the project. You need to remember back at the outline level that your story (whether fiction or nonfiction) will have branches to it. Keep track of all the branches you design, whether those branches are the result of choices the user makes for a character's actions or selections your audience makes from a menu of how-to subjects. As you plan, structure, and craft your story, think in terms of the branches you want your audience to be able to take.

Similarly, as you write the individual scenes, modules, or sections of your document, remember that they will work best if you remember the hooks that connect them to other branches in your story. In many ways, this skill partakes more of copywriting than creative writing, though it too can be as creative as you want to make it. Like writing advertising copy or descriptions in a brochure (which it may very well be, if you're designing a marketing piece for a professional client), you need to focus your sentences on the present subject, at a very tight level of detail.

Yet in addition to hitting the salient points of each scene, you need to focus on how each module will fit with the remainder of the story. That will tell you what links you need to create to make each scene grab onto the hooks of other related scenes. You'll also know which

Director cast members you need to use as the buttons, menus, and other control options for your document, and what frame you want to appear when the audience clicks on a button.

Remember that the Lingo basics we've covered here represent about 10 percent of the language's available statements. The scripts in this chapter are in some ways the barest minimum of introductions to the power of Lingo. However, they're also everything you need to know to put hyperlinks into your Director document, and to do so in a way that presents a very natural, aesthetically pleasing document that looks less like a computer program and more like the thing you're describing.

CHAPTER

8

Output for Distribution

How do you plan to get your message out to your audience? For many of you, the answer will automatically be CD-ROM. But what makes CD-ROM the natural choice? Are there other options that might help your main product? Could some of these options become viable presentation and packaging techniques in their own right? Can they get you new customers or help expand your audience?

In truth, you have a number of delivery and distribution options. This chapter discusses the following ways of getting your message out to the audience you've identified:

- On CD-ROM or diskettes, which let you distribute fully interactive Director titles up to the size limit of the media

- On VHS cassettes, which give you a potentially huge installed base but one with no interactivity beyond start, stop, and rewind

- On the Internet and the World Wide Web, which give you a no-cost publication medium for a subset of the information in your Director title

The limitations, costs, and capabilities of each will dictate your choice of the appropriate option. However, to use these options wisely, you should consider their capabilities in relation to the audience you want to reach rather than solely on the basis of what they can and can't do.

Marketing Decisions

"Marketing and distribution decisions need to be part of your product design from the beginning," says Margo Komenar, specialist in multimedia marketing. Margo is a consultant for the Multimedia Developer's Group (MDG), and was the primary author of *Going*

Global: The International Marketing and Distribution of Multimedia (Multimedia Development Group, 1994). I recently discussed with Margo some of the main concerns that multimedia title developers face, especially if they hope to reach an international market. She provided this list of questions that title developers need to ask themselves as they begin the design phase; that's when you need to start considering your output. The answers included here combine Margo's advice with examples from my own experience to give you some idea of what to ask yourself all the way through your title's development cycle.

How carefully have you considered your target audience?

Factors such as age, gender, education level, and social issues make a huge difference in the success of a title. From my own experience and as a very general rule, adults tend to be more directed in their use of multimedia products, while children tend to be more willing to play without a sense of purpose or effect. A title oriented for young children should have a number of playful, unexpected interactions, even if it's primarily educational in nature. A title for adults should have more information about where you are in the document, how to get around, and what in general is going on; kids tend to be much more inventive in making up their own story structures to fit the images they see, while adults are much more cautious and often less creative (or at least less open about it). This is one example in which an audience definition—the age level of your intended user—will have a tremendous impact on how you design your title.

How can you understand what issues your audience is responding to in today's culture?

If you are particularly interested in global publishing issues, you may need to research a foreign country or culture to see what's hot there. If you're planning to release a sports title in South America, for instance, Brazilians probably don't care about the National Football League, but millions of them are crazy for information on soccer and Formula One motor racing (though that has sadly dropped since the death of their national hero, Ayrton Senna da Silva, in 1994).

How do you decide on a distribution platform? With Director, the concerns are minimal, focusing mainly on color map issues and differences in transitions. But the standard answer ("why, the PC, of course") is entirely wrong for the educational market, where the Macintosh is far and away the dominant platform in the U.S. In fact, at a recent multimedia publishing forum, the audience was given a surprising piece of information about the number of CD-ROM drives in the world. While it's generally quoted as 12 million and growing, one of the publishers made the point that the number of CD-ROM drives that have been correctly installed are working properly and are regularly in use are probably closer to 4 or 5 million—and most of those are probably inside Macintoshes. So in spite of the 80 percent-plus market share that DOS PCs have in the worldwide installed base of personal computers, remember that other concerns may drive your choice of a delivery platform in an unexpected direction. Be aware, do the research, and keep your options open.

The Advantages of Using Bundled Products

Consider a variety of bundling deals that can increase your awareness of a product's capabilities. For example, buyers of SyQuest cartridges have been treated to several megabytes of clip art and even some Macromedia Director clips. The added value of such a bundle works in both directions: SyQuest gets to distribute useful content on their cartridges, and the providers of the clip art get a wide distribution. You probably don't want to include your entire title for free on a CD-ROM, but you can include pieces of the title or include some of the graphics. Conversely, if you plan to set yourself up as a consultant and developer of multimedia titles, you may wish to include an entire, short title as a sample of what you can offer your clients.

SyQuest isn't the only option, of course. Most print publishers are scrambling to stake out a piece of the electronic media market, and you may be able to find a publishing company with an interest in doing joint ventures. Print media still have tremendous value, as I hope you'll agree after paying for this book; there are many options available to you as a multimedia developer through which you can provide additional value on paper. If you produce entertainment titles, in particular complex games, you might find a good two-edged market in tip books or in providing novelized versions of the story leading up to the events in your multimedia title. By two-edged market, I mean that it's a benefit that cuts both ways. Sales of the multimedia title can help improve sales of the book, as long as the book provides more information about how to enjoy the multimedia title better. Conversely, sales of the book can help improve sales of the multimedia title, because the book can increase awareness of your multimedia product. Likewise, videotape versions, particularly of training courseware, can extend the market for your multimedia product, and they're very easy to develop from a Director movie.

You know the options, but how do you make informed decisions? The next section offers you some guidance in this area.

Choosing the Right Distribution Media

Once you study your audience and the subject matter of your presentation, you'll have a good start on deciding which media work for your Director title. Instructional video cassettes can easily incorporate Director into the transitions, titles, text fly-ons, and other effects. This is especially true when the cassettes are used in combination with either traditional video editing equipment or with digital video editors such as Adobe Premiere or Avid Video Shop. With enough memory and processing power, you can literally make anything from a reading instruction tape series to a music video on your Macintosh or PC, using Director to provide animation, synchronization, and effects.

The issues here include not only how your audience intends to use your product, but also how you've structured the information—in a linear way or in a modular, interactive form. For example, videotape is almost exclusively linear in nature. That is, it's theoretically possible to shuttle the tape back and forth to the point in the production where your subject of interest is located, but it's rarely worth it. Beyond the "instant replay" approach, where the user wants to see something one more time, videotape is the least interactive medium mentioned so far. So when deciding on VHS as a medium, consider these questions:

Is your product primarily linear in nature? Can you organize it to work well when all the user can do is start and stop it? Many instructional cassettes work well in this structure, where the audience can stop the cassette, try their hand at whatever the cassette teaches, and then continue with the next lesson.

Does your product rely on interactivity, such as selecting options from a menu or clicking on characters or objects in the scene? If so, you're only going to work with some kind of digital medium such as CD-ROM (or disk, if the images are simple and don't take up too much disk space). If you're doing a commercial or professional training series that's meant to be stored on the company's file server for use by employees at client workstations, all the issues about interactivity apply.

What kind of computer or computers does your target audience typically own or use? If the answer is none, then VHS is probably still the most viable option, as the video player is almost as ubiquitous as the television. For example, in the multimedia project I just completed at Cherry Chase Elementary School in which 27 first-grade students did reports on how animals adapt to winter, we made the finished reports available on VHS cassettes to be able to reach every student in class and to give them all something they could proudly show to parents and friends on television. Our presentation took up nearly 3MB of file space because of the images the children had generated for their reports. The linear version of the presentation took about 15 minutes to play through, which is about one-eighth of a VHS cassette. The classroom version, running on the computer on the school's Open House night, was fully interactive. All of the children were able to select their names from any screen in the presentation. They were then able to use the television monitor in the front of the classroom to show their work to parents and friends. But even though the interactivity was an important part of the classroom experience, we shared the children's work with a wider audience by distributing it on VHS.

Establishing Selection Criteria

Remember that the issues of interactivity and noninteractivity are secondary to the concerns of storytelling, of reaching your market, and of delivering your message. Don't publish on CD-ROM just to say you can; don't add interactivity just because you want to see how it works. Interactivity adds tremendous potential for involvement, immersion, stimulus, and educational value to a piece of media. It can let students or players feel more in control of the situation than they do as a passive viewers. However, badly designed interactivity— either in the form of a poor user interface or of interactivity simply slapped on the product, like ketchup on an angel-food cake—will do more harm to the product than leaving it out entirely. Don't do what's neat or new: do what's right, and what works for the story and the effect you want to achieve.

Having said that, it's probably a good bet that most of you are interested in producing interactive titles with sufficiently complex structures and sufficiently rich media that you need the CD-ROM's combination of interactivity and mass storage capability. Most likely, disks, VHS cassettes, or even the World Wide Web (discussed in a few pages) will be secondary distribution paths for you. This is particularly true if you're looking to produce a consumer media title for eventual sale in bookstores, software stores, and other consumer media outlets. If you're using Director to develop a title for in-house use, such as a training piece for deployment on your organization's own local-area network or a classroom presentation to be used by students, VHS is a great way to provide materials that can reinforce the on-site learning experience with at-home follow-up.

CD-ROM Production

For those of you looking to produce and sell a commercial Director title, there really are no alternatives to CD-ROM publication today. The other media discussed in the preceding section let you offer potential buyers a taste of your product through a medium that's accessible enough, inexpensive enough, and easy enough to generate that you can use it as a marketing tool rather than as a production tool. For this reason, I'll concentrate on CD-ROM production and the associated costs and technical issues.

Cost Issues

The cost of producing on CD-ROM has been falling for some time now, so most of the prices here should be taken as snapshots of an industry in transition. To understand the context for these prices, you need to understand the issues involved in that transition.

The two forces that have been driving the cost to produce CD-ROM have been the cost of the mastering equipment and the number of vendors in the market. From 1993 through early 1995, prices of the mastering equipment have continued to fall, which has made it easier for new vendors to enter the market. At the beginning of that time, buying the equipment for producing a CD-ROM required an investment of close to $40,000; at the beginning of 1995, trade magazines were testing CD-ROM mastering equipment that cost as little as $2,000.

Media costs vary, however, depending on what stage of the CD-ROM production cycle you're in. The low-cost CD-ROM mastering equipment, called CD-Recordable (or CD-R), requires a "gold" disk for which the raw media cost is about $15. This is obviously not feasible for mass distribution; it is the equivalent of making plates in the printing world. The gold CD-R master disk lets you test your title on all the machines you plan to sell it for, and it also lets you produce copies for between $1 and $2 each, on mass-production equipment. Most CD-ROM production still involves contracting the job out to a service bureau, which is an independent vendor who takes responsibility for producing the individual units that you plan to distribute.

Today, the situation is analogous to creating camera-ready copy (CRC) for a book or brochure, which a printer then duplicates for publication. Most professional printers will produce your CRC from raw materials and strip in text and photographs if they're still working the old fashioned way. If they are more up to date, they will work directly from electronic files. Likewise, you also have several options when using a service bureau to produce your CD-R. Depending on the setup of the service bureau you select, you can deliver the electronic masters of your Director title in any of the following ways:

- Make your own master copy on CD-R if you have the equipment in your own production environment

- Deliver your files, fully structured and ready to be duplicated, in some other electronic medium such as SyQuest, magneto-optical (MO) cartridge, or even tape (still popular as a backup medium)

- Carry in your computer or its external hard drive, from which the service bureau can extract the information you want to publish

■ Send your files via modem to the service bureau

■ Transfer the files over an Internet connection, using the Internet's file transfer protocol (ftp) if that is available to you and to your service bureau

Of these, making your own master copy on CD-R costs the most because you need your own CD recorder, though prices there are falling dramatically. In return, you will have the most control possible over where files are located, what they're called, how they're structured, and how they appear on your final CD-ROM. Does this mean you have to spend $2,000 or more for your own CD recorder? Only if you want that control.

A good service bureau will work with you to give you the control you need, at reasonable costs. At time of publication, the going price for producing a CD-R gold master disk runs between $125 and $175, depending on the amount of data you want to publish and the amount of work the service bureau has to perform to get the master disk done. For your first CD-ROM production job, that's an incredibly low price for the education you'll get. Interview several service bureaus and find one that's close to your office or studio and one that's willing to walk you through the steps involved in producing your title. Aside from the costs involved, there are a number of technical issues you need to address when you're preparing your electronic media for publication, and a service bureau that is willing to work with you in advance can save you money and trouble in the long run.

Technical Issues

In some ways, a CD-ROM is just a very large floppy disk that you can only write on once. In other ways, it's a new medium altogether. One of the most important ways in which CD-ROM is new is that you can reach both Macintosh and Windows platforms with the same publication. You can also reach Unix workstations, but at present there is no way of playing your Director title on a Unix system without an expensive, and generally slow, emulation system. It's technically feasible, but the economics aren't there to justify it for most Director users.

Your market definition will have revealed whether you want to reach a cross-platform audience; if you don't, then your CD-ROM is in fact just another recording medium and you only need to set it up according to the normal directory and file structure in the platform of choice. Remember, however, that your audience will not be able to move files around within that structure, so if you have any dependencies between files, you will have to structure your directory in the correct way before you produce your CD-ROM. If any file in your eventual title needs to look for another file on the disk surface to find a video clip or a separate Director file, for example, this would constitute a dependancy between files.

Two Important Buzzwords: ISO-9660 and Hybrid

To understand how you produce a cross-platform CD-ROM, you need to learn two new buzzwords: ISO-9660 and hybrid. These terms refer to a pair of digital publishing standards that will let you produce a single piece of media that you can insert into either a Macintosh or a Windows PC to play your title. The difference between the two standards is that a CD-ROM published under the ISO-9660 standard presents a single file system that both the Mac and the PC can share; a hybrid CD-ROM has separate file systems for each platform. Why choose one or the other? If all your media is compatible across platforms (such as flattened QuickTime movies, for example), use ISO-9660. If you plan to distribute executable files that only work on one platform, make a hybrid disk. In short, hybrids are either, ISO-9660 is both.

How this appears to the user is that an ISO-9660 CD-ROM has one directory structure in which there are files visible to the Macintosh and the PC, whichever one happens to have the CD-ROM installed in it at that moment. Your job as the media producer is to make sure that any incompatible files are clearly indicated. For example, Windows (or technically speaking, DOS) uses file names of eight characters, followed by a period and three more characters (the last three are called the extension); you can't include a space in a DOS file name. The Macintosh can have file names up to 31 characters long, with embedded spaces. In an ISO-9660 CD-ROM, DOS will have trouble with Macintosh file names if you use them for any of your content; in a hybrid CD-ROM, there will be completely separate structures for the Macintosh and the Windows files, so the names don't matter.

What does this mean for Director files? With Director, you need to create the playable file—the Projector file—on the platform that you want it to use. Each Projector is its own executable program, which uses your images, text, and flow information as its data. And because executable programs have to be coded in different ways for different processors, you can't run a Macintosh Projector on a Windows PC. However, you can edit and work on your Director files on either platform, but chances are you don't want to distribute your files only to people who already have Macromedia Director. This means that you really need either a hybrid CD-ROM or a completely separate CD-ROM pressing for each platform. If you choose an ISO-9660 format CD-ROM, you'll need to supply duplicate media (Projector files and all other executables) for both platforms. This being the case, you might as well choose a hybrid format to begin with, as it provides the familiar structure of each platform's environment to your users.

Printing to Videotape

In comparison to preparing for CD-ROM publication, printing to videotape is simple and straightforward. You hook the adapter from your Macintosh or PC to the VCR, press Record, and start your program. The hard part is selecting the adapter. There is a huge variety of digital-to-analog conversion systems available, starting around $200 with the LTV card from and extending well into the $4,000 range with the Radius VideoVision Studio or RasterOps MoviePak2 Pro Suite.

What's the difference for your money? The Radius setup will let you do broadcast-quality digital video: full-screen, full-motion, with a studio-quality breakout box that combines a high-resolution video digitizer with video-out. The LTV card intercepts the signals from your CPU to your monitor, converts them to analog NTSC, and lets you hook that up to a tape recorder or NTSC monitor.

Preparing the Presentation

There are some things to remember when you prepare a presentation to go out on video—or for that matter on any television monitor. You should understand the importance of interlacing, color, and image size.

About Interlacing

Thin horizontal lines on the computer don't translate well to TV. This is because of the way that computer screens and television screens handle images. Computer screens draw their images pixel by pixel, as though creating a mosaic out of tiny tiles one by one. More significantly, computer screens create their images all at once, refreshing the entire screen in a single pass. On the other hand, TV screens use a technique called *interlacing*. Interlacing causes the TV monitor to draw only the even-numbered lines across the screen in one pass, taking ⅟₆₀ of a second to do so. Then in the next ⅟₆₀ of a second, they draw the odd-numbered lines. On images shot with equipment designed for interlacing, there's no problem because the input and the output are designed to work together.

On images prepared on computer, the difference between interlacing and noninterlacing screens can cause problems with lines that are only one pixel high. A sharp, narrow line that shows up clearly on the computer will flicker on and off, at ⅟₆₀-second intervals, when you play it on a TV monitor, because half the time it's there and half the time it isn't. The solution is to make sure any horizontal lines you draw for playback on a TV monitor (whether for use in a presentation room or on videocassette) are at least two pixels high.

A Few Words about Color: NTSC Video

Color is another concern. In the U.S, the broadcast standard is set by the National Television Standards Committee, and is therefore referred to as NTSC video. NTSC video and computer displays use different mathematical models for mixing the signals that create color in each of them. When you hook a computer to an NTSC monitor, there's a good likelihood that the colors will appear different. Common problems include flicker from too-bright colors, or colors that are darker than expected. This of course is in addition to the problems of digitizing color to begin with.

Briefly put, digitizing hardware introduces "noise" in the darker colors. What the eye (or the analog video camera) perceives as a smooth gradation of colors, or even a single color in the case of shadows and other dark areas, the digitizer sees as falling on one side or the other of a numeric boundary. The eye can distinguish in excess of 80,000 colors (though human color perception varies from individual to individual); a digitizer that creates (or a monitor that displays) 8-bit color images is limited to 256. This shows up most strongly in dark images; where the eye detects colors mingled too closely to individuate, the digitizer groups all related colors into the same numeric value. This shows up in what has been described as a "paint by numbers" effect in digitized video.

What this means is that you need to design presentations for video using colors that will look good in NTSC, and use a high-quality digitizer connected to a system that supports enough color depth to use 24-bit color (what's called Millions on the Macintosh Monitors control panel). Yes, you can tune the monitor as you play back your presentation. But it won't record that way. Can you expect all your customers, users, or potential prospects to adjust their monitors to make your title look that good? Designing the right colors into the document from the beginning, and using a high-quality, high-performance digitizer will produce better results no matter what the output or publication medium.

Understanding Overscan and Underscan

The third problem involved with printing to videotape relates to the image size of TV and computer monitors. Two more buzzwords come into play: underscan and overscan. These terms refer to the size of the image area within the picture tube of the display device. Most computers use *underscan,* meaning that there's a black border between the monitor's cabinet and the part of the screen used to display information and interact with the computer. Most televisions, on the other hand, use *overscan,* meaning that the outer edges of the image are actually hidden behind the television cabinet itself.

This difference can cause problems if you display an image that has information in the corners or at the edges. For example, I recently hooked an Apple Macintosh PowerBook to a television, using the E-Machines Power Presenter system. While I could see everything on the PowerBook's screen, I couldn't see the Apple icon at the top left of the monitor on the TV monitor. This caused no problems for me, but it illustrates how much screen real estate you may lose to overscan. You can design around this if you know about it in advance; don't put crucial information too close to the edges of the screen, as it may disappear on some TV monitors.

Disks: Small Files, Large Installed Base

Compared to videotape, disks are very simple to work with when it comes time to distribute your title. The only real restriction about using disks is the amount of data they contain. It's easy to fill up 1.4MB of information once you start feeding in video, complex graphical images, and other media-rich presentations.

The answer is in compression software. Two popular packages are StuffIt for Macintosh and PKZIP for Windows. Both packages have similar effects: They allow you to "squeeze" your data and program files so that they take up less room on a disk. Better yet, they allow you to split a single file across multiple disks, which makes it possible to distribute files larger than 1.4MB without resorting to CD-ROM. For example, the Windows version of Director that I have was distributed on disks rather than on CD-ROM. However, it may not be economically feasible to use disks. One rule of thumb puts the break-even point at two floppies. That is, if your media, program, or data is large enough to fit on two floppies, it's still less expensive to distribute that way. If it requires three floppies, you save money by going with the CD-ROM. (And for the sake of completeness, one CD-ROM can hold more information than 450 floppies.)

Cost might not be the only consideration you have in mind when considering floppies. For starters, they're still more widespread than CD-ROM drives; if you want to be sure you reach the widest possible audience, floppies will work in more systems than CD-ROMs will. Because of this, floppies make a good way to distribute complimentary materials, samples, or other information extracted from your primary title. You may find it worth the time to develop an electronic brochure or handout to give people who want to learn more about how your primary title or service works.

Electronic Distribution Options

You can also consider distributing your title, or at least portions of it as teaser information, through dial-up connections or on the Internet. You have three basic choices:

- Have your potential customers dial up your own modem and operate as a bulletin board service (BBS)

- Let Internet users have access to your information through the Internet's File Transfer Protocol (ftp)

- Publish an interactive tour of your title, in modified form, on the World Wide Web (WWW)

Despite the convenience of using dial-up connections, you should always keep in mind that there are inherent risks in letting users have access to your electronic information. The first, of course, is that they can do this without paying for it. While it's great to be recognized for your contributions to a field, it's also great to be able to pay the rent. If you plan to operate a BBS as a profit-making venture, or to put your company's products on electronic display, you'll need some way of managing the electronic transactions required to do business this way.

Doing Business the Electronic Way

As I write this, SmartValley (a coalition of government and commercial institutions in the San Jose area) is developing a research project called CommerceNet for the specific purpose of identifying and solving the problems related to doing business over the Internet. Briefly, the problems include verification and security: You need to know who the customers are, and both you and your customers need to know that nobody else will be able to intercept the transaction.

At present, CommerceNet is a promising prototype of a new way of doing business electronically. When it becomes a fully proven solution, it will revolutionize the way you distribute multimedia and the way you get paid for it. For now, however, you simply need to take precautions to make sure your transactions will be secure in both directions. That is, you have to assure your customers that their credit card numbers can't be intercepted if they order that way, and you also have to be certain that your customers can't break into your own file system.

The World Wide Web

No doubt you've heard of the World Wide Web (WWW), the structure that exists on the Internet for browsing hypertext and multimedia documents from any spot on the globe. It's one of the hottest technical subjects around these days, and with good reason: It's an essentially no-cost way of publishing interactive information that combines audio, graphics, motion, and text; or rather it puts all the cost onto the shoulders of the people who dial up to read your documents. The World Wide Web (or Web, for short) promises to be a revolutionary way of distributing information as it matures and as Web browsing software—the programs running on individual workstations around the world, from which people read information elsewhere on the Web—becomes available and adds performance.

The fundamental unit of information on the Web is the page. This is a "virtual" page rather than a physical one, with no actual limits. You should probably work to keep your pages structured so that they contain most of their information in an area that fits in a single 14-inch monitor. While your readers will be able to scroll up and down through longer pages, the ability to encode hypertext links into the body of your Web page means you can set up information structures with links, road maps, and other navigation tools as described in Chapter 1.

Here are three questions and answers about the Web that you may find useful:

Is the Web suitable for multimedia title distribution? Probably not as the exclusive means of distributing your title, but it's a great way to get the word out, let people play with samples, and possibly add a distribution channel to the more traditional methods of sales and marketing. You might want to make it possible for people to buy your title in an electronic catalogue, then download it from your Web site after they receive a key that lets them use the software at their own site. The technical issues required to implement such a licensing scheme are far beyond the scope of this book, and have nothing to do with Director, but if the idea appeals to you, it's definitely something to look into in one of the nine billion books on the Web that have been published recently.

Can you run a Director title on the Web? No. The Web displays text, GIF-format graphics, and digital video; it permits hypertext links both in text and in some graphics. Because of this, the Web can provide a great way to offer people a short clip and a little interactivity, plus some text that explains what your title is about. Think of it as a cross between a magazine advertisement with unlimited page space and a videocassette with a one-minute time limit.

How much does a Web page let you include? As a practical limit, most Web developers (using current technology, so this will be out of date sooner than the concerns about designing for human interaction) find that a 5MB video clip is about the maximum people will tolerate. If there's much more video, it takes too long for people to access the files when browsing the Web. As a practical limit, using 160×120 (¼ NTSC) windows and 15 fps, this is about a minute's worth of noninteractive QuickTime video.

You can of course include more than one video clip in your Web page; they don't take time until the user decides to look at them. Because of the time delay involved in sending the images to the end user, you need to be particularly careful about describing your video clips so that your users will be able to identify them fairly clearly from the descriptions. And you can make hyperlinks to the video in multiple locations in your Web page.

Technically, the choice for video for the Web is probably QuickTime as this is compatible with both Macintosh and PC. Save your Director movie as a QuickTime file by using the Export button of the File menu. Also, using the xanim program, you can play QuickTime movies on Unix workstations running the X Window System. To run QuickTime movies on non-Apple systems, you need to "flatten" them using MoviePlayer 2.0 or an equivalent program. This creates QuickTime movies that can run on Macintosh, Windows, and Unix clients.

One proposed use of the Web is as a means of giving your potential customers a sample of the media, the "look and feel" if you will, of your title before they pay for it. With careful planning and thought to the interactivity and to the video clips you include, you can use the Web as a way to introduce your Director title to a large group of people, by letting them see some of the content for themselves.

Laser Disc: High Quality, Low Volume

I haven't spoken much about interactive laser disc, for one simple reason: It's one of the last media that most people are interested in using for the multimedia titles they ask me about. But every so often, I'll encounter someone who wants to produce or to purchase interactive video on a laser disc.

If you haven't been thinking of this medium yet, it's probably not for you. The distribution of interactive laser-disc players is still fairly limited, so as a mass-market medium it doesn't have the impact of CD-ROM. It requires just enough added expense, complexity, and difficulty for most people to use it that it hasn't caught on to the degree of CD-ROM.

But within laser disc's niche, its adherents are committed to the format. The main reason it inspires such enthusiasm is the quality of the image and the speed of playback. Because it's not running on a CD-ROM drive but rather was developed for home entertainment use, the laser disc player can transfer full-screen, full-motion video in all the popular formats (at least NTSC and PAL), with better image quality and far less degradation than VHS tape.

The two markets that rely heavily on laser disc are education and retail kiosk development. In education, there's a popular package called MediaMax that lets you control a programmable laser disc player from a Macintosh. MediaMax is an extension to HyperCard, containing XCMDs (external commands) that operate a number of standard interactive laser disc players. Through MediaMax, teachers can prepare video sequences for use in lectures and discussion groups. And there is a surprisingly large selection of educational laser discs available for use in the classroom.

If you have an interest in laser disc video, be prepared to spend a lot more on the process of preparing your video images. You won't be able to take advantage of a laser disc's extra image clarity unless you use better quality video equipment, better digitizers, better connectors, and of course better technique. They also cost slightly more than CD-ROMs to produce because there aren't a thousand entrepreneurs out to make a killing in the laser disc market, as has happened in recent years with CD-ROMs. The actual cost of the player is minimal, and can be built into the cost to develop the public access kiosks.

Kiosk Applications

The other application for which laser-disc video is often chosen is the public-access kiosk. Laser disc's high image quality and sharp detail makes it possible to use broadcast-quality video images, with far better smoothness and much richer colors than CD-ROM permits.

I recently learned about a public-access kiosk that effectively uses a laser disc video. It provides information to visitors at a state park in California. A laser disc was the right approach because the audience includes people who have high expectations of the quality of the video. The developers felt that CD-ROM quality video, at 160×120 pixels and 15 frames per second, would not provide sufficient image clarity, smoothness, or detail for the audience they were expecting or the image the were presenting. It's worthwhile to remember that while many computer users are excited to have any video coming from a CD-ROM into the monitors, the general public's main experience with video is on television.

The Future

What's out there waiting for us in the area of output distribution? I'll start with two completely safe predictions: higher density and lower cost. These are safe because in the first place, several competing companies are now struggling for mind-share in the marketplace over their new super high-density mass storage standards, which are between six and ten times as dense as a CD-ROM today: 3.7 gigabytes on a little piece of Lexan isn't something you sneeze at. The only question now is which format will be the Beta of the new industry, and which will be VHS. Neither of these is in widespread use yet, and all of what little discussion I've read on the subject gave no indication of when the technology would start to proliferate.

Predicting costs is only slightly less safe. Sources in both the Intel and the Apple worlds have told me to expect CD-Recordable units for around $500 within a few months of this book's publication. This is an exciting prospect, because it means people with the money to buy a mid-range laser printer can buy a CD-R (CD-Recordable) device and premaster their own CD-ROMs.

CD-Recordable is an intermediate step between disk and CD-ROM. You can write on it only once in each location, but a multisession CD-R lets you update it several times before it's completely full. (Think of it as a notebook in which you write in ink.) Today, the media cost for a blank CD-R disk is about $15. If the market in home CD-R drives does what the market in laser printers did when they were introduced, the prices for these blank disks should drop significantly, as economy of scale makes it possible to reduce manufacturing costs.

If you plan to do a lot of CD-ROM recording, it's probably worth your while to spend the $2,000 to $5,000 that a decent CD-R machine costs. At the lower end, the CD-R device installs into your Mac or PC, or sits on the table beside it. This means it takes up the computer's entire processing capability while it's writing the CD-R. The fastest writers today can copy 660MB (the size of a standard CD-ROM) in under 20 minutes. The more expensive CD-R units today are stand-alone devices. Before you buy, make sure you know which one you're getting.

When this book is first introduced to the stores, CD-ROM technology will be a publishing technology, controlled by corporations and others with the money to invest in the machinery to produce it and the network of distributors required to get CD-ROMs into the stores. Within a year, CD-ROM technology (and here's the wild prediction) will be a pervasive, grass-roots technology similar in breadth and ubiquitousness to desktop publishing. The day isn't far off when the church newsletter will be produced in Macromedia Director and handed out on CD-ROM. I'm currently working to put a school newsletter out electronically, and if that works we'll take it to the school district.

On the one hand, this means great things for repressed artists and film producers, who will now have the capital to set themselves up with a digital multimedia studio. On the other, it may well lead to a period of chaos as people inexperienced in design find themselves in charge of a video camera, graphical layout tools, and a copy of Macromedia Director.

CHAPTER

Game Theory and the Importance of Play

When I was in the sixth grade, my class started a math unit on fractions. Our teacher began to go over one of the operations that required inverting fractions. "Does anyone not know what inverting means?" she asked; a fair number of students raised their hands. She then asked a student named Mark to come to the front of the classroom. The teacher then lifted him off the floor, flipped him over, and said, "This is what 'invert' means.

"You will never again forget what it means to invert something."

Sometimes the best way to involve the emotions in a situation that doesn't seem to call for them is simply to stand that situation on its head. In the process of working with Director to develop titles, you may discover that if you can involve the emotions, people will learn and remember far more effectively than if you don't. This final chapter presents you with some guidelines for understanding the significance of learning and playing within the context of developing multimedia titles. It also provides useful tips for using Lingo lists to construct groups.

When Is Play Appropriate?

It's my somewhat provocative notion that play belongs everywhere; the trick is finding the appropriate level, type, and method of play for the context. Educational software designers often talk about finding the "sweet spot," or the point at which fun and learning balance out in developing edutainment. Kids want to play Super Mario Brothers, but when they're using computers in the classroom they need to learn geometry or social studies or reading. Where do you find the sweet spot between learning and play? Or to put it more succinctly, when is play appropriate, and how much play is appropriate?

Most of the answer will come from your understanding of your audience, their expectations of your title, and a sense of sympathy with your subject matter. By sympathy, I mean a sense of appropriateness between the subject and the manner in which you present it. It's one thing to build an amusing, playful title about mathematics or reading, both of which are serious subjects. It's quite another to develop appropriate methods of play in a historical title about a period of conflict, war, or oppression. With careful thought, you can still make a title about slavery or the Thirty Years War emotionally engaging, even compelling, by building in appropriately sympathetic mechanisms for play, such as storytelling and role-playing. A multimedia version of *The Diary of Anne Frank* could let the audience choose to be one of the characters in the story and follow his or her actions over the course of the book as a way to identify with the way World War II affected the lives of individuals.

Remember as well that there are very different kinds of play for different audiences, as well as for different subjects. In a kid-oriented title like one of the popular Living Books series from Brøderbund, it's entirely appropriate to have silly, unexpected, comical results from clicking on the characters on each illustrated page. A title designed to teach adults to read, on the other hand, must avoid any hint of childishness or patronization of its audience, but that doesn't mean it can't involve play. Adults play many kinds of games—from card games and board games to sports and action games. The sense of structure, concrete instances of abstract rules, and a sequence-oriented approach to playing games is very similar to the structure, concreteness, and sequence required by learning.

The Relationship between Playing and Learning

One crucial component of play is unpredictability—when you don't already know the outcome of an action, because of an element of chance in the mechanism of play or because of an element of skill. There's a kind of apprehension about the outcome; it's a pleasant apprehension, to be sure, but in all forms of game-playing the player pits his or her stake in the matter against the unpredictability of the outcome. In games of skill, the unpredictability comes from one's own control over the mechanisms of play, whether that means throwing a football or clicking the mouse in time to shoot an alien out of the sky. Additionally, in games against opposing players or teams, the skills and choices of the opponents add an element of unpredictability beyond each player's own innate abilities. In games of chance, the unpredictability comes from the random elements in the method of play: the order of cards in a shuffled deck, for instance, or the number that comes up when the player rolls the dice. But because it's play, the apprehension about the unknown is tempered by the pleasure of the game itself (at least for most of us).

Now, let's look at learning. Learning occurs when someone takes an action for which they don't know the outcome; in fact, they take an action in order to discover the outcome. Learning involves retaining a sense of the connection between the action and the outcome—the stimulus and the response—so that it's repeatable, but in the early stages the outcome of the action is unpredictable. Play, of course, also involves retention of the connections between the player's action and the response within the structure of the game; the player retains a sense of the connection between when to swing the bat and how far the ball goes. Learning, however, often has an unpleasant sense of apprehension, associated with embarrassment over getting the wrong answer.

Studied in this way and looking at these criteria, then, it's apparent that the mechanism of play and the mechanism of learning are almost exactly the same—taking an action in the face of apprehension that is designed to produce an unknown response. If you can tap into this mechanism for your instructional titles, you can bring

the power of play to the need for learning in ways that are unprece-
dented. How can you accomplish this objective? Here are several
tips for adding an element of play to an educational, instructional,
or other professional title.

**Ensure a close sympathy between your subject and the
method of play that you choose.** As mentioned earlier, you need
to find an appropriate kind of play for your subject, as well as for your
audience. Audience analysis and needs assessment will help you get
past this point of your document's design. You need to bear in mind
your audience's age level, skill level in the subject, and level of appre-
hensiveness in the face of computer-assisted training or education.

**Consider a role-playing model for your player's interac-
tion with the title.** Role-playing games by their nature evoke a
sense of identification with the character in the play. Point-of-view
shots, for instance, give an immediacy to the game that watching
characters interact cannot provide. You may not be able to use an
entire role-playing format for your title, but look for ways in which
you can let your audience take on the part of a character in your
title. By encouraging this kind of association between the player and
the character, you make it easier for your audience to make the
emotional bond between themselves and the subject matter. If they
care about someone or something in your title, they may care more
about learning the subject.

**Where appropriate, use storytelling techniques rather
than documentary narrative style.** Storytelling techniques
stress showing rather than telling about an event or a realization.
Basic creative writing classes have always focused on using dramatic
action that demonstrates your characters in the middle of conflict,
rather than telling your audience what happened. For training titles,
don't just use a simple example to demonstrate something; put it
into perspective within the context of your audience's intended use
of the product or service you're training them for. If possible, give

your audience believable characters (and make them take on the role of one of these characters, if this is in any way feasible) in some kind of situational conflict, then let your audience resolve the conflict.

Consider that people learn from failure, not from success. "We all learn from our mistakes" is a common enough adage, but you can use it to your advantage in designing how your multimedia title responds to incorrect or suboptimal responses on the part of the player. If you're teaching someone through your title, an incorrect response deserves much more attention than a correct response. An incorrect response can mean a number of different things, ranging from basic ignorance of the topic to confusion over the way the choices were presented. Incorrect responses are a good place to begin your storytelling support sections; when a user picks the wrong choice, have the guide, mentor, or narrator interact with them to help reinforce the mental structure of the information you're trying to convey.

Help your audience discover the answer rather than giving it to them. If you want your users to retain a lesson or a piece of information, make them work for it. Balance the play so that it's challenging enough to keep them thinking about how to proceed, while not so difficult that they don't get anywhere. What your audience can find out for themselves is much more cherished than what you hand them on a platter.

Use inventory to review and reinforce the information and lessons your audience has had. Inventory is a term used in games that involve finding and keeping objects, such as in adventure games. For example, a game that involves searching through the rooms of a deserted castle might let the player pick up and keep certain objects that might be of use, such as magic swords, maps of parts of the castle, containers of water, and the like. Some of the inventory might well be the way that your players amass points, but it's quite different from keeping score. Inventory, because it uses objects rather than numbers of points, can evoke the emotions, as well as providing strong visual cues to your player.

So if you're developing an educational title, especially for adults (such as software training or professional education), you need to remember that while the mechanism is the same as for play, the emotional context is quite different. Your job is to bring the context of education closer to that of play, by engaging the emotions and putting people at ease.

From Idea to Execution

With the above suggestions as goals, here are some techniques you can use to implement these thoughts on play in your Director title.

The simplest technique invovles structuring your title around multiple-choice responses. Once again, remember the appropriateness of play: You may not want to have these simply be choice A, B, and C from a quiz question, all in text; these can be buttons to push, doors to open, tools to pick up, or anything else you can represent with a Director cast member. If you were creating a software training title, for example, you might have a reproduction of the program's tool bar, from which your users can select the appropriate icon for the operation in which you're training them.

You should make sure that the Lingo script is associated with the sprite rather than with the Cast member, however. Consider the tool bar example just mentioned. You probably want to reuse the same cast member each time you show the tool bar, which will be at least once for each button on the tool bar. But the response your users need will vary depending on the context of the lesson you're teaching. For instance, if you're working on an exercise teaching users how to print a document, the Print tool bar button is the right one for your users to select. But, if you're working on an exercise for importing a file, the Print button is wrong. You want different Lingo scripts attached to each button depending on the context. In the first example, you want the Print button's script to send your users to the frame that tells them they are correct. In the second example, selecting the Print button needs to send your users to the frame in your title that reviews the function of the Print button. By associating the Lingo script with the sprite instead of with the cast member, you can change the operation of the sprite's script in every frame. This way you can use the same cast member for each button, but let the sprite script direct your users to the appropriate part of your lesson.

Exploring Different Play Metaphors

There's some discussion now in the industry about the metaphors that we support for play. In this context, the metaphor is the way you use the mouse, keyboard, or other input devices to select something on screen that represents another action. At present, computer games support these three basic metaphors for interaction:

- The sports metaphor: hitting a ball, running, jumping, kicking, or otherwise performing the sport that the game is simulating.

- The combat metaphor: blasting away at alien invaders, enemy aircraft, or whatever the game's story presents.

- The mystery or puzzle metaphor: typically adapted from text-based adventure games, the mystery metaphor involves exploring an environment while searching for clues to the mystery.

Additionally, I'd like to propose a fourth metaphor that I haven't seen used much: A role-playing metaphor in which the player takes on and identifies with a personality. While this is used to some degree in sports, combat, and puzzle games, the role-playing metaphor can be successfully adapted to educational and training games, as long as you keep in mind the sense of sympathy between the player and the subject. A game that tells your players "Let's pretend you're an enchanted princess" isn't going to be effective in an interactive training piece designed to explain leveraged buyouts to MBA students. However, the MBA students might be very motivated and engaged by a play scenario that has them taking on the roles, actions, and characters of the CEO of a mid-sized corporation involved in such a transaction.

But whatever kind of game you choose, the trick to its success in the marketplace (or in the case of educational titles, its success as a teaching tool) is that it has to be fun to play. Having great media, a good sound track, terrific voiceovers, and even a great story line won't compensate for a game that's simply boring to play.

How do you know whether it's fun to play? The first test is fairly simple: Does it light you up? Does it make you go back even after you've designed it, tinkered with it, debugged it, and reworked it? You need to be honest enough with yourself to know when and whether the play mechanisms you've selected are working. Here are some additional considerations for adding fun to your title:

Avoid repetitiveness. If the same scenes come up over and over again, think about how you have structured your game. This is somewhat different in puzzle games, because your players may go back over the same ground many times in search of new clues or while mapping an area. But in action-oriented games, you need to vary scenes, characters, and the actions that your players take to advance in the game.

Use patterns, but vary them. Action games in particular, whether sports or combat games, frequently use patterns of response that let the player know what's going to happen next. The patterns are a beneficial part of the game's overall design in one way, because the recognition of them is a tremendous reward to the player: It gives them a sense of control and power over the situation to know, in a science-fiction oriented combat game, that the attack

begins with three alien cruisers, followed by nine alien star destroy-
ers, and finally the flagship of the mother fleet. Such knowledge,
however, can quickly make the same patterns become boring.
Consider changing the sequence depending on how long the player
has been at it. And of course, the speed and complexity of the patterns need to increase as the player advances to the next level.

In mystery games, the patterns will usually involve the ways that
your players get around in the virtual environment you have created
for them. One way to vary the pattern is to have additional characters who are also moving through the environment, either in patterns of their own or at random, so that your player never knows
upon entering a room whether there will be a hideous, slavering
ghoul or a bloodthirsty maniac with an axe on the other side of the
door. If every door has ghouls, ax-murderers, or (if you really want to
strike terror into the hearts of adults) IRS agents on the other side,
the game rapidly becomes much less fun than if there is never a horror on the other side—but there might be. One of the most successful elements of a good mystery is, of course, the suspense, a category
that deserves its own study.

**Use suspense to keep the audience on the edge of their
keyboards.** My own favorite horror movies, to take an extreme
example of the genre, always involve much more suspense than
graphic depiction of either carnage or of the villains. Stephen King,
the most famous practitioner of the horror novel today, wrote an
essay a decade or so ago in which he explained how the suspense of
not knowing led to far more horror than the most gruesome details
ever could. When you hear something on the other side of a door, he
explained, your own imagination, fueled by suspense, can make it
out to be something truly horrible. The longer you keep up the suspense, the more time your imagination has to build it into an
unimaginable horror. In fact, in some ways it can be a let-down
when you finally reveal the horror to your audience; it changes from

being an unknown horror to an identifiable horror ("oh, it's just a ten-foot bug," to use King's example).

So it is with suspense in your Director title. Set up your scenes with sound effects, lighting, clues, and cues in the art direction of each shot or each frame that heighten the element of suspense. Let it build for a good, long time—10 to 15 minutes may not be too much if the payoff is good. Every minute that you keep your players in suspense, you're not only engaging them emotionally in the story you're telling, but you're also forcing them to use their own imaginations.

Balance the difficulty. A game that's too easy or too hard to play isn't fun. You need to make the game challenging enough, in its given metaphor, that the player has to work a little to have fun with it. On the other hand, if you make it too difficult to advance or to operate, you'll lose users to frustration. The best—probably the only—way to know how difficult or easy your game is to play is to test it with sample members of your target audience. If you're developing an educational reading game for children between the ages of 3 and 7, for instance, you'll have an entirely different set of constraints than if you're developing a mystery game for adults.

How Do You Know It's Fun?

Earlier in this chapter, I suggested that your own judgment is the first way you can begin to determine whether your title is fun to play (or to play with, if it's not explicitly a game). That's an important initial step, but the most important question is whether members of your target audience enjoy playing it. The only way to be sure of that is to invite a number of them in and let them use your product. Listen to their feedback; you don't need to do everything they tell you, but you should listen for trends, for consensus, and for common areas of criticism and praise.

The phenomenal success of Robyn and Rand Miller's *Myst* has spawned a number of imitators, and much discussion in the CD-ROM and computer game community. Probably *Myst*'s most recognizable feature is the richness of its media: the eerie sound effects, the detail of the three-dimensional scenes, the textures of objects, the colors and lighting of scenes. I made a number of screen snapshots of different places on Myst Island to use with my screen saver, just because I loved looking at them; I wanted to have the library, the reflecting pool, and a few other places show up when my monitor was idle.

But the imitators haven't enjoyed the same sales as *Myst* in spite of being comparably rich in the visual media elements. More than one game developer, in describing one or another of the subsets of these Myst-like games, has expressed the opinion that the games themselves just aren't as much fun to play. They simply don't engage the emotions to the degree that the story of Sirrus and Achenar does.

I've already proposed a number of ways you can inquire into what makes your title fun, or what could make it more fun, to play. I'd like to stress that the suggestions are really best expressed as questions rather than as answers. Every title is different (or should be), and there is almost no way of issuing categorical statements about all titles in a genre without lapsing into formulas for their creation. But the following questions will help you keep your focus on the play aspects of your title:

Does your title have a rhythm to its play? Look at the patterns you may have used to set up your users' interactions with your title. Is there a rhythm to them, something that your players can grow to recognize and use to help them achieve control over the play? This holds true for educational and professional titles as well; if you're developing college-level courseware, don't check out of the discussion just because you think this is kid stuff. Rhythm can also be the pacing of scenes, of dialogue, and of dramatic action; it can be the balance of visual imagery to dialogue and narration. It can even be alternating between a big-picture overview of a subject and detailed discussions of individual issues.

Do you vary that rhythm to keep it interesting? This also holds true across the board. Too much of the same rhythm becomes singsong, useful for short mnemonics but irritating in long structural components. In straight-out games, of course, you need to vary the rhythm of play to keep the element of surprise and unexpectedness in the way your players interact with and are involved with your title.

Are the explicit uses of your metaphor appropriate for your audience? Don't let this lapse into stereotyping of the people you hope will pay money for your title, but do make sure that the ways you've implemented your chosen metaphor are appropriate for the age group, educational level, language skills, and other quantifiable aspects of your audience. For example, the enchanted princess versus CEO discussion of a few pages back offers this insight: If your audience is primarily made up of girls between the ages of 7 and 10, it's stereotyping to decide categorically that they'd only be interested in playing the part of the fairy princess. However, it's probably not appropriate to their education to ask them to take on the role of a CEO involved in a leveraged buyout—but that doesn't mean you can't ask them to be the boss of a company. The difference is that probably few 7-year-olds of either sex or any economic stratum have been exposed to the concepts of leveraged buyouts (and I admit that I'd have to do a good deal of research to describe it myself!), or could explain that CEO stands for chief executive officer. It's not that the metaphor is necessarily inappropriate for the audience, but rather that this explicit use of the metaphor doesn't work with the people you're expecting to buy your title.

Does play happen in the imagination or only in the eyes? This is my way of distinguishing special-effects games (and movies and TV shows) from story-oriented games (and movies and TV shows). It's too common today for people to dismiss "this generation" as having no imagination. Many believe that kids today have lost the ability to generate their own involvement in stories, that television and video games have shortened their attention spans and made them lose interest in anything that isn't graphical and explicit.

While much of this is true, I don't believe the imagination has been lost; I think it's merely been atrophied. You, as the developer of multimedia titles, have the key to reviving that atrophied imagination. Engage the curiosity, fill your audience with wonder—give them something that works at a deeper level than simple shock value or shoot-and-explode gratification. You can't change the world back to the way it used to be, but you can make something new that's better than the past or the present. And one of the most important keys to that future lies in engaging, strengthening, and nourishing the imagination.

Teaching the Imagination

We've looked at elements of learning and elements of fun. Now it's time to start combining them in the titles you're developing in Macromedia Director. To recap, here are the main elements of learning:

- People learn by taking an action that has an unpredictable response; the apprehension involved in the unpredictability is often unpleasant.

- People learn from mistakes more powerfully than they learn from successes.

- People learn by constructing a mental model of the information, then by having that model reinforced by subsequent information, either new or reviewed.

The elements of play include the following:

- People play by taking an action that has an unpredictable response; the apprehension involved in the unpredictability is usually pleasant.

- People enjoy play when it balances a predictable rhythm with surprising details.

- People play by projecting their own personalities into the stories, characters, and actions of characters in the medium of their play.

It's time to look into ways to combine the two ideas. Begin by assuming that you have people making mistakes. The mistakes might be in a learning title, where the players take choices that don't achieve the response they want; in a game title, a mistake might mean that the monster eats you, or the aliens blow up your spaceship, or you sink into the swamp. In either case, the mistake provides an opportunity for the player to learn—either to learn how to play the game better, or to learn how the subject of the educational title actually works.

Now consider what happens in an educational title when you structure interaction with the title in such a way that players are able to project their own personalities into the stories, characters, and actions in your title. The educational title takes on a crucial element of play. Furthermore, if you then structure your title so the character makes minor, correctable mistakes regularly, you invoke this powerful mechanism for learning in a context where the player has already made an emotional connection to the character. Finally, make some of the responses unpredictable—don't make your character lose at every turn, but don't make the patterns inviolable either.

Most important, make your title tell a story that involves the player in the characters with whom they can identify. The story elements will show up in every aspect of your Director title, from the backgrounds to any video you shoot and down to the way you structure cast members and sequences of frames.

Using Inventory Inventively

We've talked about how inventory is the gaming term for the stuff you get as you play a puzzle or adventure game. It's also a useful way to keep track of your players' progress through the game. Instead of having your players' scores represented by so many points when they get something right, try having them build something and get a key component for each thing they get right. Better yet, have them not know what the thing they're building will do when it's done—build in a little pleasant apprehension. They'll work all the harder to figure out what the heck this contraption does, and they'll be much more present to solving the problems that you set for them.

What other fun things can you put in the title? You can require that your players progressively learn how to use one goodie in a title before they can go on to the goodie at the next stage. Just remember to make up a structure and build toward it.

Lists in Lingo

Lists are the mechanism by which Lingo lets you construct groups on the fly. For example, you would use a Lingo list to maintain the inventory for a character; as your character acquires objects in the course of play, or as your character passes different levels of play, you can add elements to the list that tracks accomplishments or possessions. Here's how it works.

The most explicit way of creating a list in Lingo is to use the list() function. (You can also create lists by putting the items on the list inside square brackets, but explicitly using the list() function makes it clearer when you need to debug your Lingo code later, or if you bring in new team members to work collaboratively.) To create a list, you set the value of a variable to the output of the list() function, as follows:

```
set inventoryList = list("gold", "silver", "platinum")
```

When your movie executes the Lingo script containing this line, subsequent Lingo scripts will be able to use the variable inventory-List, which contains gold, silver, and platinum as its members.

Because inventory is something which your players add to during the course of play, you will probably want to create the variable early in your game, typically during the initial stage as your title loads and prepares for execution. This way, all subsequent executions of Lingo scripts can read, add to, or replace values in the list. To add an item to the end of a list, such as when your character picks up an object in a mystery game, use the following structure:

```
append inventoryList, "rubies"
```

After executing that statement in a Lingo script, the variable inventoryList contains gold, silver, platinum, and rubies.

If your player spends his platinum, you can update the value of inventoryList to reflect the absence of platinum by using the deleteAt command:

```
deleteAt inventoryList, 3
```

This changes the contents of inventoryList to gold, silver, and rubies. But note that the deleteAt command unconditionally removes the list member at the position represented by the second argument to the command—in this case, the number 3. If you execute the script containing the example shown here a second time, it will once again delete the third element in the list. If you execute the script on a list containing fewer than three elements, you will get an error.

You need to structure your lists carefully if you want to use them for the more ambitious uses I'm going to suggest next: creating

interactive elements from different pieces of inventory that your players pick up along the course of your game. But this will give your players a way of visually representing the inventory they acquire, and if this inventory further represents and reinforces knowledge that they have been exposed to during the course of play, the visual representation you can create can add playful interest to your title while also maintaining an education-oriented structure within which your players can learn.

Lists in Pictures

To present a fun, interactive way of representing what your users have acquired—whether physically as a result of the game, or intellectually as a result of the educational aspect of your title—consider a simple example such as how to assemble a tricycle. You could structure your title around different modules that included assembling the pedals to the front wheel, assembling the fork and handlebar to the frame, installing the seat, and connecting the rear wheels to the platform at the back of the frame.

Your navigation screen could serve as a review screen as well by following a structure such as this one. In your initialization, you need to create a variable containing the list of sections your player has finished:

```
set finishedSections = list()
```

This creates the variable finishedSections, but leaves it blank. Now, each time your player completes a section of your movie, you could add an element to the list of completed sections with a statement such as this:

```
append finishedSections, "pedals"
```

This adds the word "pedals" to the end of the list contained in the variable finishedSections. Subsequent Lingo scripts can look at the variable finishedSections and know which portions of your document the player has already completed.

What can you do with this information once you have it? You can use it to display a piece-by-piece illustration of the tricycle when your player displays a list of completed sections in the document. Here's how you need to structure your presentation.

In the frame that displays the entire tricycle, you need a separate cast member (and therefore a separate sprite) for each of the components you handle in individual sections of your title: one for the pedals, one for the seat, et cetera. When your player selects this frame, you can display the components corresponding to the sections your player has finished by making the following tests for each of the sections:

```
if (getOne(finishedSections, "pedals") = not 0) then
set the visible of sprite 5 to TRUE
end if
```

In this Lingo script, the getOne function returns one of two values, depending on whether or not pedals is in the list finishedSections:

- If pedals is in finishedSections, getOne returns the number of the position that pedals occupies in the list. For example, if it is first, getOne returns a 1; if it's fifth, getOne returns a 5.

- If pedals is not in the variable finishedSections, getOne returns a zero.

The following line determines the visibility of individual sprites in your frame. This example assumes that the cast member for the pedals has been put in channel 5 of the Score window:

```
set the visible of sprite 5 to TRUE
```

This statement makes the sprite associated with channel 5 visible. (Don't get confused and think that the sprite number is associated with the Cast member number—sprites are associated with the score and the stage, not the cast.)

Using a structure of Lingo scripts like this lets you reinforce your users' knowledge by showing them what they've already learned, as though it was inventory in an adventure game. Additionally, by showing them the pieces as they fit together in the finished product, you reinforce their structural understanding of the subject.

In addition to a tricycle, you could use this scheme to display states or countries in a geography game. Players could learn and be quizzed on details about individual countries in southeast Asia, for example, and as they get the countries correct they could refer to a frame containing a map that showed them the countries they had identified correctly.

Conclusion

The most important thing to remember about Macromedia Director is that your customers, players, and users expect multimedia to be fun. Even if you are working on a straightforward reference title or corporate procedures training document, multimedia and Macromedia give you the power to make it fun. Always remember the sense of pleasant apprehension that differentiates fun from fear.

Pictures, video, animation, and sound effects all have their role in making a title successful. But most important is the overall design, the choice of what appears in each screen and what happens as a result of interacting with the components on the screen. This requires planning, strategy, and executing your title in an orderly way. You need to have a vision and implement it, tracking pieces of continuity along the way.

I've demonstrated a few techniques for using individual portions of Macromedia Director in ways that the company documentation can't mention. Likewise, I hope you develop your own uses that go beyond the examples and suggestions I've included in this book. Never forget that at this stage in the history of interactive entertainment, every title has the potential to change the direction of not only the multimedia industry, but of human communication itself. Play big, and challenge people to live up to your own standards rather than living down to theirs.

APPENDIX

A

Computer-generated Animatics: Storyboarding Tools

Who Uses These Prototypes?
Prototype Development Software

Traditional animators and creative people working in the advertising business are familiar with the animatic, which allows them a way to produce quick, proof-of-concept art. An animatic is similar to an intermediate animation technique called a "pencil test"; it is a specific kind of prototype that lets you run the basic idea past other people who may not have the same vision you do of the product.

When you prepare prototypes for interactive CD-ROM presentations, you need to verify and test more than just the story, the look, and the pacing. You also need to verify the interactivity: the branching, the flow, and the selection of options at various points along the way. A traditional pencil test or animatic could be made by videotaping or photographing sketches, then editing them into a rough approximation of the time and flow of the finished piece. However, the prototypes of interactive documents must be tested with some provision for choosing on-screen options.

As powerful as Director is, it's sometimes easier for you to begin with a different tool that has fewer features and is less complicated to use. The question soon becomes one of knowing when to quit: How much time should you invest in a prototype that isn't made with the final tool you plan to use for publishing? Prototyping tools buy you the ability to get to the stage of testing interactivity easily and quickly. Getting to that stage quickly can be very important for interactive presentations. After all, not only must the presentations look good, they also have to work.

This appendix lists and evaluates several readily available prototyping tools that do some subset of the things that Macromedia Director does. While these programs are not as powerful as Director, they enable you to perform simple tasks quickly enough, and early enough in the development process, that you may easily save enough money and time to justify purchasing one of these simple tools.

Who Uses These Prototypes?

A prototype is a useful tool for the following three kinds of reviews in particular:

- Art directorial review

- Functional review

- Marketing/fundraising review

In each of these three scenarios, you may or may not want (or have time (or have the personnel) to use Director to develop your prototypes. If you've decided that Director is the tool for your eventual development (and if you've bought this book, that's probably a safe assumption), you may still not be far enough along the learning curve yourself to feel comfortable making a presentation that potential investors will see. If this is the case the tools I describe later in the chapter, beginning with Aldus Persuasion, make excellent ways of producing great-looking presentations (if less powerfully than Director). At the same time, you can incorporate any existing art, images, video clips, or sound files that you have developed for your Director title.

Let's take a look at each type of review in turn.

The Art Directorial Review

When you're working on portions of a multimedia document, it's important for all the team members to understand how it's supposed to look. This is part of an art director's job: to decide on color schemes, on how characters look, on what media elements you include, and on what the overall feel of the document is at various steps along the way. Sometimes, in the multimedia environment, it's necessary to produce tests that also verify interactivity, that show the flow and dependencies between sections of the document as it will eventually develop.

Much of an art director's job in a multimedia document development setting will be to keep color maps consistent, to work with the individual graphic artists to keep the style of the characters in tune with the overall design of the title, and other steps to track the development of media for the title. However, art directors need to learn to think about interactivity as well. In a traditional linear document, transitions from one scene to another are predictable, controllable, and limited. In an interactive title, when a character leaves one setting and goes to another, how will things look? Does the setting completely change the mood? How does the color, design, layout, and overall look of the new setting work in the context provided by the one that the reader just left?

In this sense, art directors need to be concerned with interactivity from the beginning. It affects the look, the atmosphere, the mood, and the feel of the document just as it affects the technical side of things. One way that art directors can track the way the document looks during development is to rely on prototypes built using the existing media, whether in wireframe form for 3D graphics, in rough sketch form for 2D images, or in digital video or digital photographs.

Because Director's interactivity requires scripting in Lingo, the art director may not want to go through the pains of learning how to script in order to see a prototype. And from the standpoint of skill distribution, the other visual artists may not be up to scripting interactivity. If you've left off hiring Lingo scripters till later in the development cycle, you'll need to use some other, simpler method for prototyping the paths, connections, and contexts that shift in your interactive document. The tools described here are simple enough for anyone to pick up in an afternoon, and in several cases provide enough interactivity to let you start testing the look and feel of your document at the early stages of the cycle.

The Functional Review

Another stage of title development at which prototypes can be valuable is functional review or usability testing. If you are developing an educational, professional how-to, or other instructional aid, it is important to start testing early to find out whether your structure and approach are effective. This means finding a laboratory of volunteers, running sample documents that incorporate some of your media and much of your overall structure, then testing the structure on representatives of your target audience.

A prototype developed for functional review typically includes a very small subset of your title's eventual content, and may not be in any form recognizable to the eventual customer. Broderbund, for example, tested a working prototype of In The First Degree (the follow-up product to their million-selling Myst) for months, involving more than 70 people, all of whom played a text-only version of the game so that the play mechanism and interactivity could be tested completely, independent of developing the media. Testing at this stage is largely looking to find whether users feel your structure is natural, sensible, and practical, and whether the document is going to help them perform their tasks. You need to generate such a test quickly, without spending much time or money on it. However, you also need the most detailed and worthwhile feedback possible from the test. In the scenario I propose here, you can probably get by without having any of the media elements you're developing for the document, but you really need interactivity. Your testers have to be able to make selections like those you plan to have them make in your eventual document; you have to let them risk choosing the wrong thing so that you can find out what the right one is. You may want to use portions of your Director document at this stage, but more likely you'll want to develop something quickly to verify the basic flow—what's sometimes called a "proof of concept" document. If you're familiar enough with Director after having read this book, so much the better; if you want to throw together more information in less time (though with less fine control over the details of timing, color, animation, and embedded sounds and video), then one of these tools can get you farther faster at this stage of the game.

The Marketing or Fundraising Review

The last area in which you might want to use prototype tools such as the ones described here is in the marketing, fundraising, or proposal stage of the project. (Actually, this stage may even occur first, before you have the money to hire an art director or the need to test your product with end-users.) Marketing your title as it gets farther along in the development phase may mean buying space on a CD-ROM such as Club KidSoft, and including a portion of your title in a slide-show format. It might be a purely linear slide show, or you might add some basic interactivity to let people get a feel for the way your title plays. You might also want to take some of the suggestions in Chapter 8 and produce a linear videotape that represents how your title looks, then send that tape to organizations that might be in the position to assist with the funding or distribution of your title; videotape is still more prevalent than either Macintosh or Windows computers.

If you're making a proposal, you probably want to have your sample on a laptop; if you're adhering to the traditional power-lunch approach, a PowerBook is a natural addition to the table. If you're inviting potential investors into your facility, you probably have a demo machine set up to run your information—which may or may not be interactive. Most proposals need to demonstrate an understanding of the audience, an understanding of the subject, a structural comprehension of what's going on, and enough skill in the area in question to be able to convince the buyer that you can deliver what you're talking about.

Prototype Development Software

Aldus Persuasion

This is my personal favorite prototype development tool. It's reasonably powerful, has good interactivity, and gives almost adequate control over timing and sound. It runs on Macintosh and PC platforms, lets you include video and import other graphics. And it has a simple, point-and-click method for defining interactivity that lets you define, change, or restructure the destinations of jumps within a single document or between multiple Persuasion files. This is the easiest tool to make decent-looking interactive presentations in.

Persuasion began as a tool for making overheads and 35mm slides to be used to support presentations in boardrooms and conference centers. As transparent projection systems and laptops became used in more intimate surroundings, Persuasion adopted the ability to drive presentations first by mouse clicks, and then later by providing actual interactivity. This background means that Persuasion comes with a number of prepackaged slide settings; titles, borders, and text specifications are all prearranged to make it easy for you to start importing content. Alternatively, you can control the color, size, font, and style of your text individually, and you can import graphical elements created in external drawing packages or in QuickTime movie or Microsoft Video for Windows form.

Weaknesses compared to Director include timing—the finest control Persuasion permits is one second, compared to Director's 1/60 of a second control. Even then, the one-second value is a delay added to the length of time required to display a slide; in practice, it takes a certain amount of time to display the slide itself.

Animation in Persuasion is also much less powerful compared to Director: You can define fly-on and fly-off of text and graphic elements; it's great for animating titles and for making graphical elements fly across the slide. You can also do transition animation, revealing the slide underneath the one on the screen and making pseudo-animation effects that way. Because the timing is so restricted there is no way of performing animations analogous to sprite animation, real-time animation, or any of Director's other powerful animation techniques.

After its easy interactivity, the most important feature that Persuasion offers is a simple way to put media elements from your title-graphics, text, framegrabbed images, and video clips in digital form-onto your slides. You can import text from word-processing documents if desired, and then set up your jumps quickly for testing the flow of interactive presentations. To insert a link, click the Jump button (the 3D arrow at the lower left corner of the tool palette, shown in Figure A.1), then position the cursor where you want the link.

Figure A.1
Aldus
Persuasion's
Jump tool

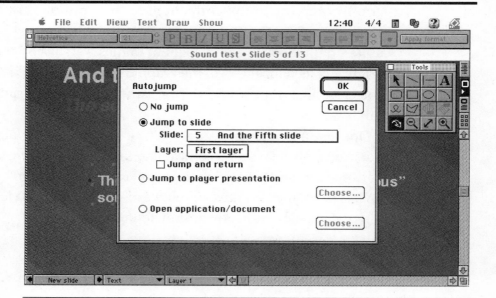

This simple dialog box makes it easy to select a slide to jump to when your users click on the screen in testing. In addition to jumping to individual slides in the document, Persuasion lets you jump to separate Persuasion documents or to external programs or application files. That last characteristic is useful because it can allow you to develop intermediate structures that actually incorporate your Director movies in the prototype. This way, if you have a team of artists and developers working on portions of your title in Director, you can still develop a quick prototype in Persuasion that uses bits and pieces of the Director document to give your reviewers a chance to see what the end product will be like.

Persuasion's interactivity is nowhere near as powerful as the Lingo programming language that Director uses, however. You must also explicitly add links to your document every time you want them; unlike Director, Persuasion has no way of tying a jump to a screen element, the way Director lets you add a script to a cast member. The next best thing if you want to use the same graphic or text to represent a button on more than one Persuasion slide is to select the graphic and the jump, copy them to the Clipboard by typing Command-C (or Control-C on the PC), and then pasting in the two units simultaneously in subsequent frames. Persuasion retains the original screen locations of the graphic (or text) and the jump, so you can add a Home button to the same spot on every slide by using this technique.

One feature that helps you do decent-looking work quickly without much effort is Persuasion's ability to specify default transitions between frames. As with Director, you can achieve pseudo-animation effects by swapping between frames in which only one element is different. To do this in Persuasion, follow these steps:

1. Display the first frame of the two in the series.

2. Select all elements on the frame by typing Command-A (or Control-A on the PC).

3. Copy those elements onto the Clipboard by typing Command-C (Control-C).

4. Create a new slide by clicking New Slide at the bottom of the screen.

5. Paste the elements you copied in step 3 into the new slide. Persuasion retains the position of the elements in the previous slide in their new home.

6. Add (or remove) the element that is different between the slide you worked on in steps 1–3 and the slide you created in step 4.

This will make Persuasion display the two slides in sequence, causing the difference between the slides to look as though it was being animated into the scene.

There are other animation techniques you can use in Persuasion, but they are beyond the scope of this book. You can also investigate Persuasion's sound handling, automatic timing, and other features after you locate a copy to test, to determine whether it will meet the needs of your prototyping tool.

Other bonuses include a royalty-free player if you want to send out prototypes to a number of people for simultaneous testing. This way you can involve people in your prototype development without having to buy copies of Persuasion for them; you need only distribute the player (which uses just over 600K worth of disk space) with your sample document and your testers can check interactivity.

In summary, point-and-click interactivity means Persuasion lets you do quick, ad hoc tests of your document's navigation, structure, and interface. The ability to import movies (QuickTime across platforms, or Microsoft Video for Windows on the PC) and the ability to link to separate applications means you can actually include any existing Director documents in your prototypes. Animation and timing controls are not fine enough, nor is drawing, for serious "intertainment" title development, but the speed and flexibility make Persuasion a great way to get your feet wet in interactivity and to plan out the flow, pace, and structure of your Director title while you come up to speed on this more powerful tool.

Microsoft PowerPoint

Similar to Persuasion in many ways, Microsoft PowerPoint lacks only interactivity, and that may change as multimedia and interactivity become more prevalent. Like Persuasion, PowerPoint originated as a slide-show tool, and it supports output to 35mm slides in the standard Genigraphic format. It also takes word processing input, following a standard outline form for text elements in each slide; one side benefit for both Persuasion and PowerPoint is that it is possible to swap in text from different languages while using the same graphics and structure.

PowerPoint lets you incorporate QuickTime movies and sound on Macintosh; OLE-enabled PCs can import Video for Windows files. Like Persuasion, PowerPoint is cross-platform. It has basic drawing tools, permits only a limited number of colors per document, and also supports the same kind of frame-by-frame animation, but as with Persuasion, only supports it at intervals of one second or longer between frames.

PowerPoint's best feature is probably the ease with which you can rehearse new timings. This feature lets you run a slide show on manual advance, while PowerPoint remembers the length of time between slides. This is great for getting initial estimates of how long things take, how much music/sound track to include, or how much you can or should talk if you're using PowerPoint as a slide presentation tool.

In some ways, PowerPoint may be best thought of as a way of producing good-looking electronic presentations to show your team members, investors, or other interested parties some of the elements you're putting into your Director title. With PowerPoint you can make attractive, clear, easy-to-read digital slides that incorporate the media elements from your title. They can only be linear—that is, you can't make a menu of options and select them from the screen, as you can in Persuasion or Director—but you can rough out the timing, flow, and context of individual modules.

Text fly-on is more limited; you can specify various effects and PowerPoint will make text buttons dissolve onto the screen, fly on from left or right, or reveal themselves one by one during the presentation. There are some basic graphics capabilities in PowerPoint, but for the most part your best bet is to import graphical elements from whatever tools you're using to develop your title—Adobe Photoshop or Illustrator, for example.

PowerPoint also has a royalty-free player, meaning that as with Persuasion you can distribute your prototype on disks, with the player file accompanying them. This lets you test your prototype with many users, getting feedback or asking for contributions of talent, time, or even money. PowerPoint also makes it possible to create short "commercials," linear pieces of the story you're telling that could include actual media from your Director title. It's a good tool for putting together fast presentations that look nice but don't have any need for interactivity or for detailed animation control.

PowerPoint runs on both Macintosh and PC platforms, though the media you incorporate have to be native to the platform on which you're running. I haven't yet tested PowerPoint on the PC with QuickTime for Windows files, so I can't say how well that works. Microsoft's Object Link Embedding (OLE) environment, the way that most Windows applications include external media, is designed to let you paste in .AVI files using the Paste Special command from the Edit menu. On the Macintosh, you import a QuickTime movie from the Import option of the File menu. This gives you the ability to publish your tests on either platform, though not necessarily with the ease that Director provides for cross-platform distribution.

In summary, PowerPoint is a fast tool for checking the flow, sequence, and timing of multimedia document components, using imported graphics that may be those you use in your eventual Director title. It supports video, audio, and slide-to-slide transitions. No interactivity means you can't test your document's structure or its branches, but the fast learning curve makes this a good tool for knocking off quick studies for widespread review.

AltaVista MediaWrangler

This relative newcomer is already focusing on a market niche as a package for developing online catalogues and brochures. It's inexpensive, simple, not as polished as Director in the way you put your presentations together, but it has a completely point-and-click interface to create links to other media elements.

Probably MediaWrangler's best feature is that it supports hot-spots (which it calls Media Area Pointers, or MAPs) of any shape with up to 255 points in the polygon. If you need to draw a hot-spot around an irregularly shaped object—such as a tree or an automobile or an article of clothing—MediaWrangler lets you do this easily. You simply draw on the screen until you have outlined the shape you want your hot-spot to have, then drag the icon of the media element you want to reveal into the MAP. It's just about the easiest way to develop interactivity that there is.

For automatic play, MediaWrangler gives you reasonable control over timing and sequencing in the MediaWrangler Pro version. There's also a powerful database utility in the Pro version; you can sort, select, and otherwise manipulate the objects in your image library by a flexible set of records that let you define relationships easily on the fly. MediaWrangler could actually be a very effective support to your Macromedia Director development, if only in the way that it lets you sort, organize, and track your visual media elements.

MediaWrangler runs on the PC only, but it supports all PC image types. It does as reasonable a job with the Windows palette problem as any program I've seen; the Redisplay menu option lets you reload the color palette for the image that has input focus (the one whose title bar is highlighted), which will clear up most ugly color issues that arise from loading another image on top of an earlier one, when the two images use different color maps.

MediaWrangler uses a Wild West motif for their user interface and other elements of the product. To keep track of images that you are using in a particular presentation, they employ what they call the Hitching Post. This is somewhat reminiscent of Director's Cast window, in that it displays a thumbnail-sized image. This is a nice touch for visual thinkers.

Additionally, MediaWrangler provides an excellent royalty-free player for distributing test copies, samples, and so on to a wide base of developers. In particular, AltaVista supports posting electronic catalogues on the Internet, and works with MediaWrangler customers to make this easy and inexpensive.

MediaWrangler's minuses are that it's not currently cross-platform, so if you use Macintoshes, or if your testing and review team does, you're out of luck. Also, it isn't intended as a slide-show presentation program as are PowerPoint and Persuasion; it's an image database, which means you can link images to one another but they always appear with the Windows border. This is good in that you can close, minimize, maximize, and otherwise manipulate them just as you can any other window on the PC. On the other hand, it means that a selection of elements in a MediaWrangler presentation can end up looking like a pile of photographs scattered on a tabletop. You can certainly do that if you want to, but it doesn't look like what people expect multimedia to look like.

In summary, MediaWrangler is easy to use, generally intuitive, works with any kind of image type on the PC, so you can import your actual media elements that you will be using in Director. PC-only means this product is not useful for cross-platform work; run-time player means you can distribute prototype versions of your interactivity to a wide base of testers. Your best bet with this program is to use it to map the links and connections between visual elements, then to sort them and categorize them using the visual database. That—and the ability to draw arbitrarily shaped hot-spots (MAPs)—is MediaWrangler's greatest strength.

HTML and the World Wide Web

The Web (discussed in Chapter 8) may be a great way to get widespread user testing, feedback, and market awareness of your product while it is still in development. In the context of this appendix, the Web is an excellent way to distribute a document that lets your users focus on the elements of your interactivity and the structure of your document.

You can include .GIF images and digital video in your Web documents, meaning you can at least show your testers or reviewers what your title will look like. You can also structure your document's interactivity in the form of hypertext links, so that your reviewers will be able to see what kinds of combinations they might run into in the actual document.

HTML is a tag-oriented text formatting technique, abbreviated from HyperText Markup Language. You can actually create your HTML documents in plain ASCII text in a line editor if you so desire, then add the commands to import and display graphical elements when your users view them on a World Wide Web browser such as Netscape or Mosaic.

There are several advantages to developing a prototype of your multimedia title on the Web:

■ Distribution costs are minimal. If you already have a Web connection, putting up a page and telling people about your uniform resource locator (URL)—the way people can browse your Web page—doesn't cost much.

■ Feedback is easy, even encouraged. Because the Web is part of the Internet, it's pretty much guaranteed that Web users can send you electronic mail. If you want to solicit responses from a wide variety of users (many of whom will be quite opinionated indeed!) about how your title looks, works, sounds, or otherwise appears to them, the Web is a great way to do it.

■ Your audience will be international. If you have any intention of marketing your eventual title in the world outside the United States, the Web gets you there now. This is a great way to find out, before you publish and distribute CD-ROMs, whether the population in a given country will respond to your title in the way you hoped.

Summary

The costs involved in producing a multimedia document are dominated by the time required to develop art work. The actual coding time in a typical multimedia development cycle is fairly short; art work can consume up to 70 percent of a title's budget. With that being the case, you stand to save significant time by releasing prototypes early in the process so that you can get feedback from users, investors, and your own colleagues. The software packages described briefly here represent a few ways that you can generate prototypes quickly, using tools that are less powerful than Director but which will let you see what your title is going to look like.

APPENDIX

B

Addressing
Common Questions

The Frame Rate in the Control Panel

The Number of Colors in Each Cast Member

The Preferences Dialog

Ensuring Color Palette Usage

This appendix addresses some of the questions that will come up in the course of working on your Director title.

Throughout this book, I occasionally mention settings, specifications, and other controls that you should verify or set before beginning to work. The following sections discuss some of them.

The Frame Rate in the Control Panel

When you first begin working on your Director document, you need to specify the frame rate. By default, Director uses the frame rate as it was set in the last document you were working on. This can hang you up if you are working on more than one title or more than one movie within a title, and your movies have different frame rates.

When you create a new Director file, make it a habit to check the frame rate first. Pull down the Windows menu and select Control Panel, then look at the frame rate.

For more information about frame rates and synchronization, see Chapter 6.

The Number of Colors in Each Cast Member

Director lets you specify the number of colors in each cast member. You need to be aware of this for several reasons. First, Director's default operation is to get the number of colors from the current Monitors setting on the Macintosh or from your current video driver on Windows systems. When you create a cast member, Director uses this setting as the color depth. For instance, if you have your monitor set to Thousands on the Macintosh, your cast members will automatically be created with the Thousands setting.

A problem arises if you (or another team member) try to edit this cast member on a different system, with a different monitor setting. You will either need to change the monitor setting to match the cast member, or transform the bitmap to work in the new setting. One of these approaches will almost certainly be wrong for the project; you need to prepare in advance for this eventuality so that you don't end up with 256-color, 16-bit, and 24-bit cast members in the same title.

If you're going to copy a group of cast members, as you might do when working on animation, changing a number of color settings can be terribly time-consuming. It's much simpler to start with the desired setting rather than having to go back and change them all later.

The safest way to proceed is to select 256 colors and specify that as the customer's requirements, then make sure that everyone in your team sets his or her monitor to 256 colors. If you require your customers to have more than 256 colors, be sure you say so clearly in the packaging.

To convert a cast member to a different color model, follow these steps:

1. Pull down the Cast window and select Transform Bitmap.

2. From the Color Depth selection box, choose the bit depth you want to use for this cast member. You can choose to transform a cast member to a 1-bit, 2-bit, 4-bit, 8-bit, 16-bit, or 32-bit image.

3. From the Palette selection box, choose the color modeling scheme you wish to use. You can select one of the following color palettes:

   ■ System-Mac—uses the Macintosh's standard system palette for the bit depth selected. If you then copy this Director file to Windows for cross-platform use, you need to ensure the color palette usage as described later in this appendix.

- System-Win—uses the standard Windows color palette for the bit depth selected. If you wish to avoid color palette conflicts with other graphical applications, you need to ensure the color palette usage as described later in this appendix.

- Rainbow—uses a sequence of colors that smoothly transition from one to the next, beginning with blue-violet and moving through the colors of the rainbow, ending with pale blue.

- Grayscale—uses a sequence of grays of increasing darkness, at a resolution dependent on the bit depth selected.

- Pastels—uses a sequence of desaturated colors (that is, colors that appear to have white added to them).

- Vivid—uses a sequence of highly-saturated colors (that is, colors with a high degree of pigmentation in them).

- NTSC—uses NTSC-legal colors, at a resolution dependent on the bit depth selected. Choose this option if you are planning to output to videotape or if you plan to use NTSC monitors for display.

- Metallic—uses a color palette designed to give metallic-looking highlights to a limited number of colors (copper, grey for silver, gold, green, and a few others).

- VGA—uses the standard VGA color palette (Windows only).

The Preferences Dialog

The Preferences dialog lets you control aspects of Director's interaction and output that have a tremendous effect on how your title will look, work, and play. To use the Preferences dialog, pull down the

File menu and select Preferences. Director displays the dialog shown in Figure B.1.

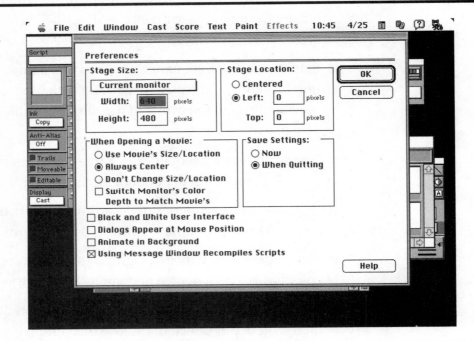

The Stage Size, Stage Location, and When Opening a Movie settings can have a huge impact on how your movie looks, and even whether or not it runs, on your customers' computer systems.

The Stage Size settings let you choose the monitor type you wish to define as the output of your Director movie. This configures your stage so that it will have the right characteristics on the monitor you specify for your output platform. In combination with the Stage Location settings, these two areas of the Preferences dialog let you control how big your final movie will be and where on the screen it will appear in the event that your movie runs on a larger screen than the one you select in Stage Size. For widest possible distribution, select a smaller monitor size such as 13-inch or 14-inch.

The When Opening a Movie settings let you specify how your movie appears on your customers' displays. The three radio buttons let you decide whether your movie determines its location on the screen, whether it automatically centers itself when it opens, or whether the Projector should never change the size and location of the movie from how you specify it in Director. The check box lets you determine whether your title should automatically switch the monitor's color depth to match the color depth you selected for your movie. You should only select that box if you are using 256 colors as your movie's depth; if you select this checkbox and you are using Millions (32-bit color depth) for your movie, only systems with 32 bits of color memory will be able to display your movie.

Ensuring Color Palette Usage

One of the most frustrating aspects of working cross-platform between Macintosh and Windows workstations is the difference in color palette usage between Macintosh and Windows programs. Fortunately, Director has a fairly simple mechanism for ensuring consistent color palette usage in your Director movie.

The Score window normally opens with the Lingo channel at the top of the window. But there are five additional channels above that: the Tempo channel, the Color Palette channel, the Transitions channel, and two sound channels. Chapter 6 discusses the Tempo channel, and Chapter 4 discusses the Transitions channel. The Color Palette channel is the one you need to use to control how your Director movie looks on Windows platforms.

You can change the color palette in use in every frame of your Director movie. This gives you the ability to use color-palette animation to change the way things look on screen, to give the appearance of motion, and also to control what colors appear when your movie plays.

The problem you need to be aware of is that in Microsoft Windows, the last program to use the color palettes "wins"—that is, its color palette persists even after the next program loads, unless that program specifically sets its own color palette. This can result in some very ugly problems if you forget to specify the colors on a PC-based Director title and you load your program after another one has run with a very different set of colors. You can end up with mustard-colored sky, purple grass, people with green and tangerine faces, and blue-and-magenta cows. It can be fun if that's what you have in mind, but I can personally vouch for how embarrassing it can be if your Director title is hooked up to a projection system in an auditorium filled with attentive, critical viewers.

To avoid this problem, you can do one of two things. It's really only necessary to set the color palette for the first scene in your Director movie; after that, the colors will use those values until you explicitly change them. (If you have really been emotionally scarred by the experience, you can always put the color palettes in every frame of your movie.)

To set a color palette, follow this procedure:

1. Use the vertical scroll bar to find the color palette channel: It's second from the top, just under the tempo channel.

2. Use the horizontal scroll bar to find the first frame of your movie.

3. Double-click on the first frame of your movie, in the color palette channel. Director displays the dialog shown in Figure B.2.

4. Choose the color palette you wish to use for this Director movie. You have the same selections of color palettes as you do when converting the bitmap of a cast member, described earlier in this appendix.

5. When you have selected the desired color palette, click Set.

Figure B.2
The Set
Palette dialog

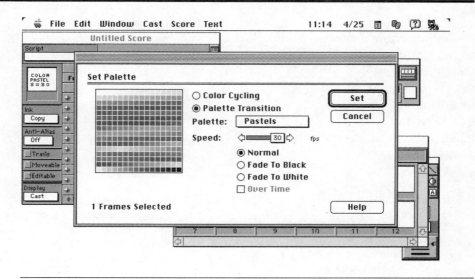

INDEX

U

V

W

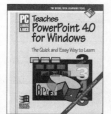

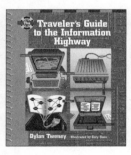

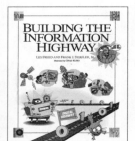

Ziff-Davis Press Survey of Readers

Please help us in our effort to produce the best books on personal computing.
For your assistance, we would be pleased to send you a FREE catalog
featuring the complete line of Ziff-Davis Press books.

1. How did you first learn about this book?

Recommended by a friend . . . . ☐ -1 (5)

Recommended by store personnel . . . . ☐ -2

Saw in Ziff-Davis Press catalog . . . . ☐ -3

Received advertisement in the mail . . . . ☐ -4

Saw the book on bookshelf at store . . . . ☐ -5

Read book review in: _____ ☐ -6

Saw an advertisement in: _____ ☐ -7

Other (Please specify): _____ ☐ -8

2. Which THREE of the following factors most influenced your decision to purchase this book? (Please check up to THREE.)

Front or back cover information on book . . . ☐ -1 (6)

Logo of magazine affiliated with book . . . . . . ☐ -2

Special approach to the content . . . . ☐ -3

Completeness of content . . . . ☐ -4

Author's reputation. . . . . ☐ -5

Publisher's reputation . . . . ☐ -6

Book cover design or layout . . . . ☐ -7

Index or table of contents of book . . . . ☐ -8

Price of book . . . . ☐ -9

Special effects, graphics, illustrations . . . . ☐ -0

Other (Please specify): _____ ☐ -x

3. How many computer books have you purchased in the last six months? _____ (7-10)

4. On a scale of 1 to 5, where 5 is excellent, 4 is above average, 3 is average, 2 is below average, and 1 is poor, please rate each of the following aspects of this book below. (Please circle your answer.)

Depth/completeness of coverage	5	4	3	2	1	(11)
Organization of material	5	4	3	2	1	(12)
Ease of finding topic	5	4	3	2	1	(13)
Special features/time saving tips	5	4	3	2	1	(14)
Appropriate level of writing	5	4	3	2	1	(15)
Usefulness of table of contents	5	4	3	2	1	(16)
Usefulness of index	5	4	3	2	1	(17)
Usefulness of accompanying disk	5	4	3	2	1	(18)
Usefulness of illustrations/graphics	5	4	3	2	1	(19)
Cover design and attractiveness	5	4	3	2	1	(20)
Overall design and layout of book	5	4	3	2	1	(21)
Overall satisfaction with book	5	4	3	2	1	(22)

5. Which of the following computer publications do you read regularly; that is, 3 out of 4 issues?

Byte . . . . ☐ -1 (23)

Computer Shopper . . . . ☐ -2

Corporate Computing . . . . ☐ -3

Dr. Dobb's Journal . . . . ☐ -4

LAN Magazine . . . . ☐ -5

MacWEEK . . . . ☐ -6

MacUser . . . . ☐ -7

PC Computing . . . . ☐ -8

PC Magazine . . . . ☐ -9

PC WEEK . . . . ☐ -0

Windows Sources . . . . ☐ -x

Other (Please specify): _____ ☐ -y

Please turn page.

6. What is your level of experience with personal computers? With the subject of this book?

	With PCs	With subject of book
Beginner	☐ -1 (24)	☐ -1 (25)
Intermediate	☐ -2	☐ -2
Advanced	☐ -3	☐ -3

7. Which of the following best describes your job title?

Officer (CEO/President/VP/owner) ☐ -1 (26)
Director/head ☐ -2
Manager/supervisor ☐ -3
Administration/staff ☐ -4
Teacher/educator/trainer ☐ -5
Lawyer/doctor/medical professional ☐ -6
Engineer/technician ☐ -7
Consultant ☐ -8
Not employed/student/retired ☐ -9
Other (Please specify): _____ ☐ -0

8. What is your age?

Under 20 ☐ -1 (27)
21-29 ☐ -2
30-39 ☐ -3
40-49 ☐ -4
50-59 ☐ -5
60 or over ☐ -6

9. Are you:

Male ☐ -1 (28)
Female ☐ -2

Thank you for your assistance with this important information! Please write your address below to receive our free catalog.

Name: _____

Address: _____

City/State/Zip: _____

Fold here to mail.   3067-18-21

_____

_____

_____

BUSINESS REPLY MAIL
FIRST CLASS MAIL   PERMIT NO. 1612   OAKLAND, CA

POSTAGE WILL BE PAID BY ADDRESSEE

Ziff-Davis Press
5903 Christie Avenue
Emeryville, CA 94608-1925
Attn: Marketing